MW00328246

WOMEN WORLD LEADERS PRESENTS

Embrace
THE JOURNEY

Your Path to Spiritual Growth

God's goodness is immeasurable
His faithfulness is secure
The joy and peace He offers
Is invaluable for sure

my story pg. 233

VISIONARY AUTHORS
JULIE T. JENKINS & KIMBERLY ANN HOBBS

©Copyright 2021 Women World Leaders

All rights reserved. This book is protected under the copyright laws of the United States of America.

ISBN: 978-1-957111-03-2

No portion of this book may be reproduced, distributed, or transmitted in any form, including photo-copying, recording, or other electronic or mechanical methods, without the written permission of the publisher, excepted in the case of brief quotations embodied in reviews and certain other non-commercial uses permitted by copyright law. Permission granted on request.

For information regarding special discounts for bulk purchases, please contact the publisher:

World Publishing and Productions, LLC

info@worldpublishingandproductions.com

www.worldpublishingandproductions.com

Scripture quotations marked NIV are taken from THE HOLY BIBLE, NEW INTERNATIONAL VERSION®, NIV® Copyright © 1973, 1978, 1984, 2011 by Biblica, Inc.® Used by permission. All rights reserved worldwide.

Scripture quotations marked NKJV are taken from the New King James Version®. Copyright © 1982 by Thomas Nelson. Used by permission. All rights reserved.

Scripture quotations marked TPT are from The Passion Translation®. Copyright © 2017, 2018, 2020 by Passion & Fire Ministries, Inc. Used by permission. All rights reserved. ThePassionTranslation.com.

Scripture quotations marked NLT are taken from the *Holy Bible*, New Living Translation, copyright © 1996, 2004, 2015 by Tyndale House Foundation. Used by permission of Tyndale House Publishers, Inc., Carol Stream, Illinois 60188. All rights reserved.

Scripture quotations marked *ESV® Bible are taken from (The Holy Bible, English Standard Version®)*, Copyright © 2001 by Crossway, a publishing ministry of Good News Publishers. Used by permission. All rights reserved.

Scripture quotations marked MSG are taken from *THE MESSAGE,* copyright © 1993, 2002, 2018 by Eugene H. Peterson. Used by permission of NavPress. All rights reserved. Represented by Tyndale House Publishers, Inc

Scripture quotations marked NIRV are taken from the Holy Bible, NEW INTERNATIONAL READER'S VERSION®.Copyright © 1995, 1996, 1998, 2014 by Biblica, Inc.®. All rights reserved worldwide. Used by permission.

Scripture quotations marked NLV are taken from the *New Life Version,* copyright © 1969 and 2003. Used by permission of Barbour Publishing, Inc., Uhrichsville, Ohio 44683. All rights reserved.

Scripture quotations marked KJV are taken from the King James Version. Public Domain.

Scripture quotations marked ASV are taken from the American Standard Version. Public Domain.

We raise a hallelujah to our Father God who has made this book possible through the power that works within each of us in an Ephesians 3:20 way.

Embrace the Journey Contributors would like to extend a "very special thank you" to each of the following for their voluntary work of love, sacrificial giving and instrumental prayer support through the production of this book.

Kayla Follin

Barbara Wert

Shelly Haas

Kelly Williams Hale

Lillian Cucuzza

Cindy Southworth

Michael Jenkins

Ken Hobbs

Women World Leaders Team of "Prayer Warriors."

Table of Contents

Introduction

"Go," the Lord said to me, "and lead the people on their way, so that they may enter and possess the land I swore to their ancestors to give them." (Deuteronomy 10:11 NIV)

Your life on this earth is a journey. Throughout the Bible, we encounter people on various journeys – Moses was instructed to go and lead the Israelites to the Promised Land; the disciples forged the way for the Christian church; and Abraham simply followed God's call, not knowing where He was leading.

One of God's unchangeable attributes is that He is faithful – we can trust Him. He was faithful to lead those we read about in the Bible, and He is faithful to lead you and me today. No matter what choices we may have made in the past, what trials we face in the present, or what obstacles we may encounter in the future, God will never leave us nor forsake us.

Our journey through life is a bit like taking a nature hike. Hiking is great, but it can also be challenging. I love hiking because it helps me get away from the hustle and bustle of the world, and it refreshes me to look further ahead than the two feet my computer screen is usually from my face. I relish taking the time to appreciate God's creation – immersing myself in the colors and the sounds of nature while being alone with the Holy Spirit and my own thoughts. But no matter how prepared I may be for a hike, unexpected twists and turns can lead to questions and uncertainty. *How am I supposed to get through this mud? Where did this trail come from – is that the way I am supposed to go? This seems to be taking forever - could I be lost?* A quick stroll down a trail can easily become a full day's adventure if I choose the wrong direction, and every path leads to a different set of choices. That sounds a bit like life, doesn't it? But I've learned that if I focus too much on the steps behind me and the wrong paths I may have taken, I miss the beauty around me and the excitement of what lies ahead. When I seek God and obediently look to Him, however, I can trust that He will connect the path I am currently on with the one He has for me, creating a beautiful journey that is mine to embrace.

Trust in the Lord with all your heart and lean not on your own understanding; in all your ways submit to him, and he will make your paths straight. (Proverbs 3:5-6 NIV)

Each of the women in this book shares the story of a path she traveled, and they all have one thing in common. No matter what she walked through and whether she ended up on her path due to someone else's choice, her own choice, or because something came against her, she embraced the journey, reached for her lifeline, and grew spiritually in the process. That lifeline was God. Each woman shares her story with you to testify that as she walked, she looked to God, trusting HIS provision, strength, and direction. And God did not let a single one down. And He won't let you down, either! God is always there, and He always has a plan to lead us to a path that is more beautiful than we can imagine.

The Lord is my shepherd...He guides me along the right paths for his name's sake. (Psalm 23:1,3 NIV)

As you read these stories, ask God to use the words in this book to lead and strengthen you. Between each chapter, we have offered you an expositional teaching, which we pray will minister directly to your heart. God has a path marked out for you, but He needs you to step boldly in faith, holding His hand and trusting His guidance as you Embrace YOUR Journey!

Julie T. Jenkins

is the Teaching and Curriculum Leader for Women World Leaders. Her duties include partnering with Kimberly Hobbs to run the ministry, writing for and leading the editing team of *Voice of Truth* magazine, and hosting 'Walking in the Word' - the biblical teaching arm of the *Women World Leaders' Podcast.* Julie also speaks at church events and retreats and serves as co-CEO and chief editor for *World Publishing and Productions* – a company that seeks to empower others to share their God stories with the world.

Born in Indiana and raised in Ohio, Julie earned her Bachelor of Communications at The University of Tulsa and her Master's of Biblical Exposition from Moody Bible College. She traveled with *Up With People,* was a long-time *Bible Study Fellowship* leader, and has completed multiple biblical and leadership training programs.

Julie and her husband Michael have been married for 25 years, live in Jupiter, Florida, and own and operate *J29 Marketing* – a full-service digital marketing company. They have three children of whom they are immensely proud.

Julie can be contacted at julie@womenworldleaders.com

TRUSTING THE LORD'S MIRACULOUS PLAN

by Julie T. Jenkins

God has a plan for your life! As children, we are often asked what we want to be when we grow up. When we are young, we dream big. But as we grow, sometimes the path can begin to look different than we imagined. No matter our steps or missteps, we can trust that God will always direct us, and if we follow in obedience, He will lead us on a magnificent journey!

My path growing up was beautiful. Although things were certainly not perfect, my environment was physically, emotionally, and spiritually healthy. When I was 18 years old, I went to college to study music and theater. I spent my high school years playing the lead in both school and community performances. I loved making people smile, and I found that my singing and acting did just that. I didn't like being the center of attention, though – I still don't! So, when I would receive praise after a performance, my response was, "Thank you! It's fun to make people smile." When I went to college, however, the acting scene was different than I expected, and I didn't like it. It didn't make *me* smile anymore. I knew I could endure four years and finish my degree, but I also knew in my heart that I couldn't work in that environment for the rest of my life.

I remember walking across campus one day during my freshman year, knowing that I had to change my major but not knowing what to change it to. As I walked past the chapel, the Holy Spirit told me to study religion. Although I heard Him clearly, I didn't even entertain the thought. I knew nothing about the Bible, despite having grown up Catholic, and all I knew about religious studies is that they were hard. Really hard. I had never shied away from anything intellectually difficult before, but I simply didn't want to "fail" at a second major, so I immediately dismissed the thought. I didn't realize it at the time, but I had just walked right past the path I was supposed to take.

God didn't toss me aside because of my wrong choice, and He didn't allow me to wander aimlessly for the rest of my life. With a tenacious calling, He kept whispering gently, leading me forward from the path I had chosen and giving me many blessings along the way.

I graduated with a Bachelor of Arts in Communications with an emphasis in Broadcast and immediately got a job at a local television station. I loved the fast pace of television news, and I excelled, soon moving from my entry-level position to working on the evening news team. In television news, the hours are tough, either very early or very late, so I was thrilled when I was offered a job at a production company. This local company, a top-notch operation, was the biggest provider of pre-packaged programming to ESPN. I began working with commercial clients and then moved to horse racing and rodeo programming.

In 1996, Major League Soccer had its first season, and the company I worked with won the bid to be the sole television provider for the league, and I became the coordinating producer. For four years, I traveled extensively and worked with the teams, the league, and the sponsors, ensuring quality production to the broadcast outlets, including ABC, ESPN, and individual local affiliates. I worked hard and was well rewarded both financially and with perks that came with being in the television industry in the '90s.

In those formative years after college, God kept working on me. He brought me an amazing husband, and a few years later, we got pregnant with our oldest child. God, even then, was laying out rocks for a path that He ordained, though it would take me years to fully recognize this. I left behind the limelight of the job I had worked so hard to achieve and became a stay-at-home mom.

As our children grew, God moved us from state to state due to my husband's career progression. All the while, God kept gently leading – giving me opportunities to learn and grow spiritually as I volunteered in different ministries and took a multitude of classes at the various churches we attended. I was comfortable and grateful for my path as a mom and wife, cherishing every step and milestone in my children's lives, never wanting to look back and realize that I had missed something. In the distance, however, I noticed other women on a different path – the path of full-time ministry – and I often thought, *Is that where I am supposed to be?* Periodically I would try to forage my way through the underbrush to get to that path, applying for jobs and taking on responsibilities that didn't feel exactly right. Through that foraging, God was preparing me for what He had ahead by giving me valuable experiences and tools.

In 2016 my husband, who had carried the family financially for the previous sixteen years, lost his job. Abruptly, the path that our family had comfortably walked for so long came to an end.

Losing a job was not unusual in my husband's field, and in fact, he had changed jobs many times over the years and was quite adept at it. But this was different. God had given us a home in South Florida, and, after years of moving, we felt like this was where we were supposed to be. And, for years, God had been growing a desire in my husband's heart to start his own business. Although we weren't prepared financially for this endeavor, we couldn't shake the feeling that there was a God reason behind the loss of his job.

The exciting thing about coming to the end of a path that God has you on is that He will never leave you directionless – we need only go to Him in prayer and walk forward in faith, trusting Him to lead. God began handing my husband rocks meant to build his new path ahead. The company He was birthing in my husband's heart was a digital marketing company. The first rock God handed us was a good friend who himself had a marketing company – G2G Marketing. The friend's name was Greg – and G2G stood for Greg To God. Greg became a business mentor of the best kind – one who has his eyes on God! The second rock was another godly friend who also mentored and guided my husband. And the third rock was a name and tagline that God gave my husband for his company – J29 Marketing, Helping Your Business Prosper. This came from Jeremiah 29:11, *"For I know the plans I have for you,"* *declares the Lord, "plans to prosper you and not to harm you, plans to give you* *hope and a future." (NIV)* When my husband told me about the name, my jaw dropped. His plan was to work from our home using what we had, including the rarely used landline that we had acquired several years earlier. The last four digits of that telephone number were 2900. To me, that was a confirmation that God had been planning to take us down this path all along!

We had to make some practical decisions to keep our family of five financially afloat. With my husband working from home, it made perfect sense for me to return to work outside of the home to provide extra income. So I started looking for a job and quickly found out that, after 16 years out of the workforce, I was not qualified for much. I went to God, thanking Him for my husband's new path, but asking Him also to lead me to mine.

God provided me with a temporary job at an air conditioning company where I covered for a woman on bedrest in her last trimester of carrying twins for a friend who could not carry her own children. I marveled that God gave me the joy to minister indirectly while also providing a small paycheck for my family. And as I refreshed my computer knowledge and learned how to develop schedules and keep financial records via QuickBooks, God was handing me rocks for the path He was forging ahead of me.

My second temporary job was at a call center, which was brutal! I've always had this thing about following rules and wanting to be liked, and I could do neither at that job. My responsibilities included making a certain number of phone calls an hour and recording answers to a survey. I was to follow the script. I kept getting in trouble for being too friendly and not following the script. That job didn't last long – teaching me that my gifts were not going to fit everywhere and reminding me that God had a specific plan just for me.

As I was working these temporary jobs, God kept reminding me that He had called me to study His Word formally, and I had now put off walking down that path for nearly 30 years. I began researching degrees, finally asking God, "Okay, what exactly do you want me to study?" I settled on getting my master's in Biblical Exposition. The path I had deemed "too hard" so many years ago now became my joy! It should have been completely the wrong time in my life to pursue a degree – we had no money, and I had less time than ever. And yes, it was difficult, but God made a way and continually strengthened me and provided for the journey.

Then God led me to a part-time job as a pastor's assistant at a church full of people who supported me and loved me. He kept giving me more rocks, continuing to lay out the path in front of me, as I learned on a much deeper level about both the practical and spiritual aspects of ministry from a completely different perspective. I worked with pastors as they developed programs, assisted as the church rebranded itself, and developed relationships with volunteers who were pouring themselves out to God and didn't mind pouring into me at the same time. God was amazingly gracious as He crafted this job, allowing me to learn and be immersed in ministry but never be overwhelmed. I could easily complete my work - always learning in the process - and then go home to enjoy my family and do my classwork. All the while, my family attended a different church where we were instrumental in planting a new campus (essentially, I now had three church families!), my husband and I led a Bible study in our home, and I continued serving in Bible Study Fellowship, where I had served for several years. The rocks to pave the path were quickly handed to me as I walked briskly, becoming more exhilarated with every step!

Then one day, God abruptly called me away from my job at the church to work at a women's ministry. A path that I didn't even know existed suddenly opened wide in front of me, and within a week, I was training someone at my old job and being trained at my new one. To say I was surprised was an understatement, but this was truly a work of God. God gave me and those around me multiple signs that this was His doing. One of the most memorable affirmations came the day I told my pastor that I would be leaving my work as his assistant. His response was a hearty laugh, which took me off guard. He quickly explained, saying, "God told me you were going to quit today. He told me in a dream. And what's more, he told me exactly who to hire in your place." Ahh...that hurt me in the flesh for a split-second! But as soon as I had gotten the confirmation from God that I was to quit, I had begun praying for someone to take my place, so I checked my hurt feelings and thanked God! Not only had He given me a new path, but He also gave me peace that I was not leaving anyone hanging when I left the path where I had been.

With my newfound skills and education provided by God, I began my work in the new ministry. It was a small operation, with only two of us in the office, but with an army of volunteers. God continued to hand me rocks as I worked with leaders from other countries, connecting with them on a new-to-me digital platform called Zoom. Within weeks of my start date, the founder and executive director had a family emergency that took her out of the office, out of town, and unable to participate fully in the ministry for the next few months. With several mission trips underway and a fundraising banquet in the works, it was time to sink or swim. By God's grace and with the work of a fantastic volunteer team, we all made it through to the end of that intense period!

Shortly thereafter, I was called out of that ministry as abruptly as I had been called into it. But I knew, beyond a shadow of a doubt, that I had been there for a specific reason and for a specific time! All along, God had a plan!

I stopped working at that ministry a few weeks before I completed my master's degree. It had been a crazy ride! My husband's business was doing well, and he had also begun working outside the home for a different ministry – God was leading him and working in incredible ways! I began helping my husband with his business, finished my degree, and offered God my services – however He wanted to use them! By this time I felt like I had been obedient and had been richly prepared. I was at peace, knowing that I had fully embraced the journey that God had unfolded before me.

Through a series of what could only be called God-incidences, I was brought to Women World Leaders. I dipped my toe in the water, but like a suction, I was pulled into full-time service for the Lord, and it was then that I saw all the paths I had been on converging into one remarkable path that God had laid out rock by rock. A path that makes me smile every day and, prayerfully, puts a smile on the face of others too!

The confidence I gained in musical theater was called upon as I stepped in front of people to teach and lead. My communication degree became vital as we began *Voice of Truth* magazine and World Publishing and Productions. My television experience became invaluable in planning our Soul Healing Summit and in editing videos to prepare for monthly meetings. The skills I learned in years of ministry positioned me to lead well through the creation of ministry departments and structures within WWL. The computer and Quickbook skills I learned through various temporary jobs are now an integral part of ministry management. My phone friendliness (not appreciated by one former job!) helps me to connect with women. When COVID hit, I was well-versed in using Zoom as a platform for connecting, which, as a result, allowed us to grow our leadership team internationally. And, of course, my Masters of Biblical Exposition pulls it all together, as the whole of WWL is focused on the Word of God, and we are ever-so-careful to ensure that God's Word is always handled correctly.

This is not the end of my story, though! I know God has more for me to do as He continues to lead me, grow me, and lays out the path before me. None of us know the end of our story, because we are still on the journey! And that is what I want you to understand as you read this book.

Each of our journeys is complex – we often can't see where we are going, and we simply cannot see the whole picture on this side of heaven. We can certainly look back and piece together how God has given us individual rocks meant to pave the path ahead of us, and that is so important to do. But until our time on this earth is finished and we can fly high overhead and get a bird's eye view of our lives, there are so many things that we won't be able to see!

You may be on a path today that is difficult - one where the end doesn't seem anywhere in sight. Or you may be walking through the roses, hoping your mountaintop experience will never end. It is the individual paths God puts us on that make up our journey. Our moments of joy, laughter, pain, and sorrow are God-given rocks purposed to form the solid ground of the path we walk. And though things don't always make sense at the time, and unrest may be heavy in our spirit, we can trust our perfect Guide to lead, provide, sustain, equip, forgive, and bless us as we walk.

As you read through this book, please know that we have prayed for you. Our prayer is that our stories, though sometimes raw and painful, will empower and strengthen you to put your eyes on Jesus, who is not only the author and perfecter of our faith, but is the One who can see all the paths and is faithful to lead and never leave you. God does indeed work all things together for the good of those who love Him, and in Him we can find the peace to walk the paths that He prepares for us. Your future is bright, dear reader, because you can trust the One who holds your future and promises to lead you.

*In their hearts human beings plan their lives.
But the Lord decides where their steps will take them.*
(Proverbs 16:9 NIRV)

EMBRACE CHRIST

by Kimberly Ann Hobbs

Remember the "WWJD" craze? If you do not, it was an insignia of just those four letters, WWJD, that seemed to appear everywhere. Some people would inscribe it on bracelets or t-shirts. Others would hold up signs at events with the letters, causing many to question the meaning. It became extremely popular in the USA. The letters stood for four important words that posed a question. What Would Jesus Do? It became widely used because it provoked thought and stood for something significant. It made people aware enough to stop and ask the question over a situation before proceeding or making a decision. It was a fun, trendy reminder that also had value.

Following the example of Jesus Christ is biblical. Perhaps we should return to that trend and ask what did Jesus do that we could embrace on our path to spiritual growth? Paul the Apostle told us to "Follow my example, as I follow the example of Christ." (1 Corinthians 11:1 NIV)

Throughout our lives, God will not steer us wrong if we look to Christ as our example and follow Him. I cannot think of a better role model to follow than our Lord and Savior Jesus Christ. As we walk through our routines, there are numerous ways to embrace Christ throughout our days. One way is to serve others as Jesus did.

" SERVE "

Then He poured water into a basin and began to wash the disciples' dirty feet and dry them with His towel. (John 13:15 TPT)

Jesus' involvement in this act of servanthood showed His heart. We can learn to embrace Christ when we follow His example of having a servant's heart. His action of washing dirty feet shows us that His inward being was willing to show humility. Think about that: JESUS washed dirty feet! The Savior of the world, God, stooped down to wash His disciples' feet! I do not know about you, but I do not particularly care for touching other people's feet, especially gnarly dirty ones. But Christ was a servant with a heart to serve well.

We can pause here a moment to reflect our own days and all the activities within them and think about how we might help others. Do we live humbly desiring to serve others above ourselves? To embrace Christ, we must accept the lessons He teaches. His actions guide us into learning and lead us by example. Part of being a servant is loving and forgiving others, both of which will most definitely positively affect your relationship with others. Jesus' example teaches us to be selfless, as He was.

As we study God's Word daily, seeing Christ's example as He lived and walked on our planet just as we do, we are reminded that life is not always glamorous or easy. In fact, when God calls you to serve, things may get uncomfortable. But, by learning to lay aside entitlement and turning toward humility, you will begin to see things from another perspective.

> *You find God's favor by deciding to please God even when you endure hardships because of unjust suffering. For what merit is it to endure mistreatment for wrongdoing? Yet if you are mistreated when you do what is right, and you faithfully endure it, this is commendable before God. In fact, you were called to live this way, because Christ also suffered in your place, leaving you His example for you to follow.* (2 Peter 2:19-21 TPT)

Do you feel; its okay to suffer, as Jesus was our example - suffer.

We have so many examples of embracing Christ that we can follow, including:

· Having Christ-like communication in our talk

· Keeping the right attitudes towards those who wrong us

· Developing others to follow Him – being a leader

· Doing everything in Jesus' Name each day

· Helping unmotivated people get motivated

· Praying for others – praying by example as He did

· Helping make disciples of Christ by teaching when you are called

Are we willing to yield obediently, following Jesus' example in all areas? If we do, our lives will show evidence of being new creations in Christ, displaying the wonders of God that will refute anything the enemy tries to rob from us. As we hold Christ near and dear to our hearts and follow His example, we can ask ourselves, in every instance, What Would Jesus Do? When we do ask that before we make certain decisions, especially those that can change the outcome of "life situations," we can trust that God will guide us. By walking with Christ daily and gleaning from His teaching through the New Testament living, we can embrace Him more and be a blessing to the world through honoring His lessons.

→ PUT OUR FAITH & TRUST IN HIM!

Kimberly Ann Hobbs

As the Founder and Executive Director of Women World Leaders, a worldwide ministry that empowers women to find the purpose which God has just for them, Kimberly Ann Hobbs oversees all elements of the ministry, including *Voice of Truth* magazine. Kimberly is the co-CEO of World Publishing and Productions and an international best-selling author, speaker, motivational leader, and life coach.

As part of "Women World Leaders' Podcast," Kimberly hosts *Empowering Lives with Purpose* each week, interviewing beautiful women of various cultures from around the world. She shares written daily devotions for WWL on the private Facebook group and on the WWL website, www.womenworldleaders.com.

Kimberly has been a guest speaker on Moody Bible Radio Stations and made appearances on Daystar Television, sharing her passion for bringing women to a closer walk with Jesus through encouragement.

Kimberly is also an artist, with much of her work reaching around the world. She sits on the advisory board of Kerus Global Education, where she helps raise support for South Africa's orphaned children, whom she loves.

Kimberly is married to her husband Ken, and together they serve in missions and multiple ministries, and run their own financial coaching business. They have children and grandchildren whom they love very much and a home-life "Tiki Hut Ministry" in South Florida.

THE BEGINNING OF WISDOM

by Kimberly Ann Hobbs

Lord, help me to be the woman who fears You and finds favor in Your eyes.

Charm is deceptive, and beauty does not last; but a woman who fears the LORD will be greatly praised. (Proverbs 31:30 NLT)

How do we become the woman of integrity God intends us to be? We wish to walk in God's excellence for our life, but it is not always easy. Personally, I can only lead by example and share with you that becoming a woman of integrity is a day-by-day journey of crawling before walking, and walking before running.

Have you ever asked God to do something major in your life and then experienced disappointment when He appeared to be working little by little rather than all at once?

God certainly has the power to give us instantaneous victories, but often some of us take a lifetime before we see the activity we want. God is going by His timetable, not ours.

Despite my sometimes-impatient behavior, I cannot imagine any place I would rather be than centered in God's presence, exactly where He wants me. As a woman free from chains and bondage, I am now walking in the excellence of the abundant life my Savior has for me,

But... it was not always this way...

God tells us in Proverbs 9:10,

The fear of the Lord is the beginning of wisdom.

Please walk back with me in time for just a moment to my childhood. I would like to create a mental picture for you as I reflect on the interior decor of my grandmother's old, cinder block farmhouse. She had countless farm animals that she permitted to roam freely throughout her home. It was a sight for anyone to see. My grandmother loved animals. She had baby animal incubators, "hatcheries," in almost every room. It was quite interesting as a child to see fury and feathered animals of different types, alive and playful amidst her cherished antiques and fine French provincial furniture. I laugh as I think back. People nicknamed her "Ma Kettle" for her eccentric way of living. It was a memory for me as a child.

In my grandmother's kitchen, standing on some old, green linoleum flooring, sat a refrigerator. It was a pudgy, moss green colored mass with two side-by-side front doors. Clutter covered the exposed greenish color. From top to bottom, newspaper clippings, old photographs, silly little magnets, and handmade presents from "us children" smothered the exterior surface. But there is one thing that stands out in my mind to this day... it was taped on the far upper left corner of the freezer door and tiny in size. It was something that remained perfectly in place on that refrigerator for 30 plus years: a teeny white paper that came from the inside of a fortune cookie. From the time I could remember---I was about seven years old---I would read the print on that paper every day that I slept at my Non's house. Each time I visited her (and I spent most of my summers there), the paper never moved. On the paper were the words typed out in exceedingly small print: *The fear of the Lord is the beginning of wisdom.*

As years passed, I photographically saw in my mind those words become larger and more pronounced to me. As a child growing into adulthood, I read that tiny piece of paper hundreds, if not thousands, of times. It became a "beacon of light" on that old appliance. In His POWER, God used that verse in my life and, even though it came from a fortune cookie, He instilled the word "wisdom" into my soul.

God had imprinted "The fear of the Lord is the beginning of wisdom" into the depths of my being. When I found out later in life that the fortune was a verse from Scripture, it became even more profound to me. Little did my grandmother realize the impact of her decision to tape up that fortune from a cookie. Her small act resulted in a child gleaning truth that would eventually change the direction of her life.

Reflecting on past stages of my life, something like "spiritual growth" had been foreign to me. I was not sure how I would get back on track to how close to God I was raised, given how far I had wandered. Unfortunately, distractions from off God's path for me consumed many years of my life. My focus was on "me" and everything else around me, rather than the God I was supposed to love and serve. But thankfully, I grew up understanding right and wrong.

When I was good, things went well, and when I was bad, I was disciplined by my parents or other authority figures in my life. There were always consequences (often severe ones) for my bad behavior choices. Thankfully, from a young age, my mom and grandmother were women of influence in my life. They taught me how to fear the Lord, an asset I would continue to use in my days ahead.

To fear God meant to reverence Him respectfully. I learned of this respect through discipline. I also learned about two forms of wisdom. There was a godly wisdom, and then there was worldly wisdom. Making wise choices by utilizing knowledge from both areas was something I needed to learn. Unfortunately, I still made wrong choice after wrong choice in my earlier life, resulting in painful consequences.

I admired wise people as I began to grow older, and I felt drawn into their conversations, gleaning the intensity of power they exemplified from their wise choices. I felt that I lacked the knowledge that would make me wise, and I so badly desired it, so I began to study the behavior of these types of people. I found myself challenged to make better decisions, and I did, but only sometimes. Still, in many areas of my life, my wrong choices continued to torment me.

Making mistake after mistake, I was crying myself through life, feeling empty and void of knowledge. I was afraid of my future. I needed God's help to become one of the women I looked up to and admired--a woman of integrity with the ability to walk through life with purpose.

Our Heavenly Father is always working for our eternal good. He is accomplishing His purpose in our lives in His own perfect way and in His own time. God's ways are not our ways, and His thoughts are not our thoughts.

God knows that little steps are better for us where we are. I believe He does not want us to be overwhelmed by situations that could happen if we experience them too quickly; He wants us to take time to learn from our mistakes. He strengthens us, shapes us, and rebuilds us from our errors of wrong choices.

As I pressed on in life, I often reflected on the fortune cookie paper. I began to pray about the word "wisdom," the word I had looked at for so many years on a refrigerator door. I lacked wisdom in my life! Yes, I may have learned a bit about this wisdom and yearned for "worldly" wisdom, having grasped only some of its meaning, but I knew what it was and wanted to obtain it, having lived among people who possessed it. I saw it in action around me, and I even held on to some of it at times, but I continued to make the wrong choices.

Until...

Lying in bed one spring day, I was extremely sick. I had been in bed for two weeks straight, suffering from a bout of severe depression. I did not realize it at the time because it was not something I had ever experienced before. I did not care if I lived or died during those couple of weeks. (I can now identify with others that this is a scary place to be.) I had made another serious mistake, a terrible mistake, but this time I did it while I was trying to walk with the Lord. So now the lament of this mistake was intensified. How could I have done this? How could this have happened? I thought I surrendered all to Jesus. It made me question myself. I was following Him, at least I believed I was, so how could this be? I was doing everything I thought to be right, but I messed up again. Why?

> James 1:5 NIV says, *If any of you lacks wisdom, you should ask God, who gives generously without finding fault, and it will be given to you.*

I never asked Him for it! It was that simple.

I needed godly wisdom; the wisdom spoken of throughout His Word.

That Word? One word. Wisdom. I laid in that bed regretting my life's choice and lamenting over another painful mistake. God had to speak to me in the darkness of that room and show me what I was lacking all along.

Prayer is the way we find God's wisdom. There is no other wisdom I wish to possess than the godly wisdom that now directs my every step in my life.

A ray of sunlight shone through a crack in the curtains as I lay in that dark room on top of my bed. The ray of light was peeping through the drawn curtain right onto God's Word, which lay open on my bed that afternoon. I had great intentions of trying to read it that day. God knew all along it would be opened to a specific page I knew nothing about.

God told me at that moment, as I glanced down at a verse the sun magnified, that I needed to pray for wisdom. He also told me I could not do things on my own any longer. I needed to ask Him for the James 1:5 wisdom spoken of in the verse that was highlighted that day.

So - I got it! I understood it, and I began to pray. For three years I made it routine, praying that prayer before my feet touched the ground each day. I asked God out loud and repeatedly for the wisdom spoken of in James 1:5. I placed that verse on mirrors in my home and on walls throughout my house. I spoke that verse back to God continuously, over and over, for months on end.

God began to reach into the depths of my soul and implant wisdom. His wisdom that He promised to give if I asked. It was not instantaneous, but it was a progression of correct choices. My daily prayers for wisdom eventually began to reveal steady progress. My life changed.

Please be encouraged that even in the tiniest of increments, God is at work in your life as you ask Him to be. Be assured He will work within you as you surrender yourself daily to Him. He will begin to work through your life and through the lives of those around you. You will find, as I did, that little by little, this will all add up to major change in your life.

Fearing God brought me to understanding godly wisdom and my lack of it. If we lack God's wisdom, we will just continue trying to get through life in our own strength and with our own understanding. This does not make for the abundant life God has for us. By lacking godly wisdom, we end up making wrong decisions and doing ungodly things.

I became so frustrated with my foolish choices it led me to pain and heart-ache. The continuous unhealthy pattern led me to the fear of what God was going to do with me. God was not punishing me, not at all; I was only suffering from the consequences of my own stupid choices, and I needed to stop. I eventually did stop when I fully surrendered and asked for His wisdom. I cried out to God for the obtainable wisdom I saw all those years on a green refrigerator door, and He began to give it to me.

Praying daily for godly wisdom became easy for me because God told me I needed to ask Him for it, and so I did. Once I did, my life changed.

Pray for wisdom. You will find yourself doing things so wise you may even be surprised. You will make a decision that turns out to be so completely right that you will be amazed. You will have insight like you have never had before. Trust God. He honors His Words.

You will begin to give sound advice to people who ask for it. You will sense danger when it is lurking. You will know when to speak and when not to speak. You will know what to say and how to say it. You will have a sense of what to do and what not to do in any situation. And please allow me to write one more thought: there is no other wisdom that you should long for over godly wisdom. It was the only thing King Solomon asked God for, and he was the wisest man in history.

As a world leader walking out her calling and growing spiritually each day, God has now led me to work with women daily. I share my mistakes openly, but I also share the wisdom God has planted and grown within me so as not to continue those mistakes. The journey I have been on of experiencing spiritual growth has led me down a path I am finding very exhilarating. God gave me a vision to lead a multitude of women, with love and encouragement, to find their beautiful purpose, and that fuels me!

As I gain godly wisdom, He continues to place me in front of women from around the world. I can pour into their lives, one by one, as God leads me through a process. The process is called spiritual growth. God is pouring His wisdom out on me, and in turn, I pour it out to others. What God is now doing is exceedingly, abundantly beyond imagination. (Ephesians 3:20)

This group of women I have the privilege to lead is spreading around the globe like wildfire across a dry field. Women World Leaders has become a movement of God with so many other wise women serving beside me. It is all by God's power working within women who are making wise choices, women who are asking the Holy Spirit to lead them each day as they serve. They are women leaders walking in spiritual growth, following the steps of Jesus, and being fully surrendered.

Anything can be accomplished when God is present. Ephesians 3:20 is my life verse. I carry it and deposit it wherever I am led:

Now unto Him that is able to do exceedingly abundantly above all that we ask or think, according to the power that worketh in us. (Ephesians 3:20 KJV)

God showed up when I asked Him to. The power of the Holy Spirit begins to work in my daily life because I ask Him to. It was not always like this. I had to make a choice, a determination to stop making the wrong decisions and ask God for wisdom to make the right ones. You can pause and ask God at this moment for His wisdom. He will give it to you because He promised He would do so in His Word - generously.

There is no time like the present to ask for godly wisdom because you are never too young and never too old. When you receive it, you will begin walking in spiritual growth each day, and in time, God's time, you will become a life-changer. No longer did I want to be a life-sucker, not another moment, feeling the life leave my body each time I made a horrible, foolish mistake. I became unbearable to live with, as you probably do when you make foolish decisions.

I challenge you to become a Woman World Leader and walk in knowledge with godly wisdom. Allow God to show you any pride that may be hiding in your life, and whenever He does, confess it to Him as sin and acknowledge Him as Lord over every area of your life.

This must become a daily reaching for you in surrendering yourself to the Lord. Ask God for the ability to see your trials as strengthening times in your life. Ask Him to make you more like Christ and enable you to handle the working tasks that He presents to you.

God gives wisdom generously to any of us who ask, and it is so rewarding. I receive daily blessings because God allows me the ability to pour wisdom out to women everywhere. It is no longer about me; instead, godly wisdom is working through me to point others directly to Him. I feel as though I live in a puffy cloud of cushion and blessings all around me. I cannot stop asking God for His wisdom each day because I would never want to think I made my "own" decision ever again. I am much more confident in life knowing the decisions I make are God's, not my own. I wish always to please Him, to be the leader walking after His heart because He is pouring His wisdom out on me as I seek Him daily. I simply pray and ask, pray and ask, pray and ask - over everything, before my day even begins.

The prayers of the righteous are powerful and effective (James 5:16); how can we deny this?

Whatever work we do as women leaders, we should want to do it well and be successful. Be diligent in all areas, and the rewards will come when you do the work God brings about inside your life.

Whether it is maintaining a home, serving at a rescue mission, committing to a ministry, or even teaching a young child to tie his shoes or caring for the sick and elderly, your reward for seeing the "results of your labor" is priceless.

Ask God for wisdom to direct you. Pray and commit your work to the Lord, and He will bless it.

> *Commit to the LORD whatever you do, and your plans will succeed.* (Proverbs 16:3 NIV)

No matter what your paycheck reflects, your work is important to God, it is important to others, and it is important to you. Do not give up. Strive for spiritual growth each day. Strive to be a woman of wisdom that others admire. Give others incentive that they can achieve this by asking it of God.

Remember, charm is deceptive, and beauty is fleeting; but a woman who fears the Lord is to be praised. (Proverbs 31:30 NIV)

~and~

The fear of the Lord is the beginning of wisdom. (Proverbs 9:10 NIV)

Become a "wise woman of God" and lead the world.

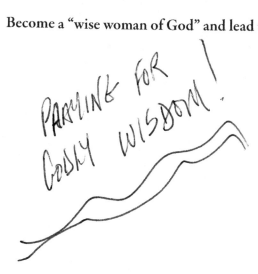

Embrace the Word of God

by Julie T. Jenkins

Many years ago, I heard a testimony about Bible study that has stuck with me. The study I was in was ending after about ten months, and the woman who stood before the microphone held a newborn baby. She said that when she began the study, she was pregnant with her first child. As a mom-to-be, she was nervous and, as a result, read everything she could get her hands on that would help her prepare for the day her newborn would see sunlight for the first time. As the months ticked by, the anticipation growing, she held firm to her study of God's Word, learning to apply biblical lessons to her daily life. And then one day, it dawned on her. God had been preparing her to be a mom through her Bible study.

The Word of God is the key to life.

In his second letter to Timothy, the apostle Paul tells us, "All Scripture is inspired by God and is useful to teach us what is true and to make us realize what is wrong in our lives. It corrects us when we are wrong and teaches us to do what is right. God uses it to prepare and equip his people to do every good work." (2 Timothy 3:16-17 NLT)

Let's take this apart.

"All Scripture is inspired by God..." The Bible is comprised of 66 books written by 40 authors over thousands of years. And yet, every single word was penned by the power of the Holy Spirit. Therefore, the teachings and instructions are straight from God Himself.

"...and is useful to teach us what is true and make us realize what is wrong in our lives. It corrects us when we are wrong and teaches us to do what is right..." The Holy Spirit works in us as we read the Word, teaching and directing us in the way we should go. There isn't a single circumstance in our lives that, approached in prayer and careful study, the Bible does not address.

"...God uses it to prepare and equip his people to do every good work." We all need instruction! The woman who gave her testimony above certainly had her work cut out for her as a first-time mom! Life is not a cakewalk, but there IS an instruction book. However, like any instruction book, we have to open it and spend time reading it to receive the full benefit.

The Word of God was written for you. You don't need a biblical degree or specific training to understand it; you simply need to trust that God will meet you where you are. Psalm 119:130 assures of this, "The teaching of your word gives light, so even the simple can understand." (NLT)

Start with a Bible, a pen, and prayer. Read a section of scripture and then journal, asking yourself:

- What are the facts?
- What can I learn?
- How does this apply to my life?

Commit to daily study of His Word, and God will be faithful to speak to you. You can trust that as you go, you will grow!

· ·

Kayla Follin

is an entrepreneur and creative spirit who aims to serve God through every facet of her life. She is a graduate of Liberty University, where she studied Graphic Design and Photography. She now works as a freelance Graphic Designer and Wedding Photographer.

Kayla has a heart for women's ministry and for using the creative talents that God has given her to provide biblical resources to women across the world. She is the Graphic Designer for Women World Leaders, responsible for the design of *Voice of Truth* magazine and all published material from World Publishing and Productions Company – including the book you are holding! Kayla also serves on the Women World Leaders' Leadership Team and Board of Directors.

Kayla is from Virginia, USA. She loves to travel and enjoy the outdoors. Her favorite place to be, and where she feels closest to God, is in the mountains, especially enjoying a windows-down drive on the Blue Ridge Parkway. She has a passion for film photography and loves to capture the personality of each place she visits through the medium.

STREAMS IN THE WILDERNESS

by Kayla Follin

My final year of college was one of the most challenging years of my life thus far. That's not usually what you hear because, for most people, senior year is an extraordinary time filled with fun, friends, and maybe a little bit of carelessness. However, my senior year definitely did not happen how I planned it. In fact, it quickly made a turn to be quite the opposite. There were so many things that I did not understand and that I would never have chosen for myself.

I remember mid junior year feeling this longing in my spirit to experience grief. I still don't quite understand it, but I just kept feeling as though I had never experienced true grief where I could only rely on the Lord for sustenance. So one day, I finally said, "Lord would you show me what true grief is like?" A bold prayer, right? Little did I know that a few months later, the world would go into lockdown for what would become a global pandemic.

Suddenly, practically everything I enjoyed was taken away. There were no events at school, classes were completely online, and there were times when I didn't leave my apartment for weeks. It was isolating, the political and social unrest became exhausting, and the concern for my family and friends was

— CALVARY CHAPEL VS CHURCH

frightening. My time in college was wrapping up, and there was no sign that things would go back to normal. It honestly broke my heart. I remembered that little prayer I had prayed a few months prior and thought that surely this was the grief I had asked for! So, I adjusted. And I let go of the expectations I had for my senior year. I surrendered my plans to the Lord and trusted that He was still good even in all of the craziness, and His plan was still sovereign. My Type A brain and ultimate planner tendencies came to a place where I was okay with the loss. Looking back now, I know that would only be the start of a year of grieving.

As the months went on, society adjusted to the new normal. I was finishing my last year of school and decided that I would still enjoy my final year despite all of the changes. I was coming out of my grief, knowing that God had taught me so much about His faithfulness. Just as things began to feel normal again, I was hit with another devastation. The relationship that I thought would lead to marriage ended without warning. Once again, every plan I had dreamt of was crushed like shattered glass. I suddenly lost all sense of direction. Then, piece by piece, every plan I had made for post-grad life slipped through my fingers. I was losing grip on one thing after another and was left feeling empty-handed. I struggled for a while, wondering why God would take something so good away from me! I felt utterly broken, and my heart hurt deeply. The only thing that could ease my soul was time with the Lord. Once again, I remembered that little prayer I had prayed almost a year prior. The Lord was leading me into a season in the wilderness, but I didn't quite know it yet. He wanted to reveal more of Himself to me, and He had a mighty plan through all of this heartache.

I found that this idea of the wilderness kept making an appearance in several areas of my life. My church was studying it, my daily devotional was discussing it, there were podcasts about it, and even my friends brought it up in conversation without knowing of this new theme in my life. I knew for a

(WILLOW CREEK ASSOCIATION) (WILLOW CREEK)

fact that this wasn't a coincidence and could only be God trying to show me something. So I dug deeper into the symbolism of the wilderness in Scripture.

The book of Exodus tells of the Israelites' journey out of slavery in Egypt. This book is filled with glimpses of God's character and faithfulness, yet mankind's failures and disobedience. The term Exodus is derived from the Greek word *Exodos* meaning "the road out" or "departure." It is a rescue story and one in which God would make Himself known to the Israelites. If you haven't read the book in full yet, there are many backstories to understand, so I highly recommend you do! In a quick summary, the Israelites are under severe oppression and in slavery to the Egyptians. God promises Moses that He will set the Israelites free and lead them to the Promised Land. Through a series of ten plagues sent by God, Pharaoh finally commands them to leave, setting them free. So the Israelites begin their journey to the land God promised their ancestors hundreds of years prior. It isn't to be an easy journey. In fact, the Lord leads them through the wilderness where they face trials, but God provides for their every need through His streams of faithfulness.

The Lord does not lead the Israelites to the Promised Land via the most efficient route. In Exodus 13:17-18 (CSB), we read, "When Pharaoh let the people go, God did not lead them by way of the land of the Philistines, although that was near. For God said, 'Lest the people change their minds when they see war and return to Egypt.' But God led the people around by way of the wilderness toward the Red Sea. And the people of Israel went up out of the land of Egypt equipped for battle." The Lord leads them to freedom, but the path is not easy! My logical and analytical brain screamed when I read this. *What do you mean He took them through the wilderness toward the Red Sea??? Why would you head toward the Red Sea and not take the most efficient road? That makes no sense!* How in the world would they successfully escape the Egyptians by cornering themselves at the banks of the Red Sea. This was surely a death sentence! But Moses, being open and willing to receive God's direction, trusts that following where God leads would be the safest path for the Israelites. And despite the Israelites resistance, He obeys God's commands.

So often, we see things as black and white. We see the safe route and the challenging route. But God sees all of His thousands and thousands of plans for every human being perfectly intertwined into one beautiful story of His creation. Things aren't just black and white for God. We can try so hard to figure out what He is doing, but His understanding and vision are far beyond what we can even comprehend. But that is the beauty in it all. He requires our trust in order to work out the beautiful redemption story He has in place. He has a purpose in everything He does!

The second half of verse 17 gives us a little bit of insight into why God led them to the Red Sea. It says that God did not lead the Israelites through the land of the Philistines because He knew that they would change their minds and return to Egypt when they saw war. He knew that they had not yet developed complete trust and dependency on the Lord's plan that would enable them to head into battle without fear. God knew that once they sensed any tribulation or struggle, they would head back to Egypt, to what was familiar. Don't we do the same?

We know when things aren't necessarily good for us. We know when we are living in our own little versions of slavery to the Egyptians. Yet when we feel called to drop those chains of slavery, we can be so afraid of the difficult journey ahead that we allow that fear to cripple us, keeping us bound. We may muster up the courage to leave that toxic relationship, stressful job, or crippling addiction, having faith that God will deliver us. Still, when things get rough, we again take refuge in the things we know and with which we are familiar. We go right back to those things that we were trying to find freedom from in the first place!

As I sit and reflect on all of the things that were taken away during my final year of college, I realize they were all just distractions. They were distracting me from the true growth in Christ alone that needed to happen. Those accomplishments, relationships, and comforts were all good, but they were keeping me from the pure communion with the Lord that my soul longed for and deeply needed. I tend to trust in myself too much, gripping on to whatever I can control, afraid that God might take it away. And taking away those distractions is exactly what God needed to do for me to learn how to trust Him fully, surrendering it all. Our journeys through the wilderness often feel like a tornado. We try to grip on to the things that look like they will bring freedom and a safe way out, but actually bind us even more.

God wants to deliver us from the things that hold us in bondage, just as He delivered the Israelites from slavery to the Egyptians. To us, His delivery often seems messy and unclear. It simply doesn't make sense. Why would we head towards the Red Sea through the wilderness when we can take the logical route to the Promised Land? The answer is simply this - the Lord teaches us, strengthens us, and rebuilds us as we journey through the Red Sea. God knew that the Israelites needed to learn how to trust Him fully, and He knew what action was required to produce such trust. God had to lead them through something that was seemingly impossible. He had to display His power in such a way that nothing else could be credited except His sovereignty and power! God does the same in us. He leads us through the wilderness in order to build our trust in Him. He leads us in this life through valleys and mountaintops, around curves and bends, so that we might one day fully give our hearts and trust to Him.

We shouldn't be discouraged that God allows painful circumstances to enter into our lives. He doesn't ever leave us on our own. He doesn't find enjoyment in our struggle. He is not hoping the worst for us. On the contrary, when we are at our lowest points, God fills the gaps. He provides just what we need through His lovingkindness. He stretches out His hand and reveals His heart to us by meeting our deepest needs.

The Lord provided the Israelites with several streams of His faithfulness while in the wilderness. He displayed His mighty power and protection by parting the Red Sea, allowing the Israelites to pass through without being harmed, and killing the Egyptians who were attacking them. (Exodus 14:15-31 CSB) He bestowed a pillar of cloud during the day and a pillar of fire by night to lead them in the way they should go. (Exodus 13:21 CSB) Then, the Lord provided the Israelites with flowing water after they had not had anything to drink in three days, naming Himself "The Lord that heals you." (Exodus 15:22-26 CSB) When they had nothing to eat, He provided them with manna and quail to satisfy their hunger. (Exodus 16:11-16) God not only met their physical needs, but He also met their spiritual needs as He revealed His character to them. And He comforted them in their time of need, despite their unwillingness to listen.

So, as we walk through our wilderness and feel resistance and struggle, we can trust that the Lord knows what is best for us. He guides us through trials, not intending to lead us to our destruction but to strengthen us. And along the way, He displays His almighty power, receiving all the glory just as He did when He parted the Red Sea. He desires the full affection of our souls, and He works through our challenges, allowing us to experience the true transforming power of the gospel. One of my favorite scriptures and one that has been so encouraging to me during my time in the wilderness is Romans 5:3 (CSB), "...But we also rejoice in our afflictions, because we know that affliction produces endurance, endurance produces proven character, and proven character produces hope. This hope will not disappoint us, because God's love has been poured out in our hearts through the Holy Spirit who was given to us."

During my final year of college, the only solid and sure thing was my relationship with my Heavenly Father. Teaching me that He is the only thing that can satisfy. He is the only thing that can provide what our souls need. It's hard. The wilderness is hard. It's uncomfortable. It's a lot of painful molding and stretching. It's breaking down things that are not honorable to the Lord and building up new growth that glorifies Him. But even when it hurts, we can know that our hope is in Him.

Before my time in the wilderness, I gripped so tightly the things I could control. I still try to sometimes, but now I know for sure that His plan is greater than mine, always. Who am I to think I know better? It's a defense mechanism. I have to fight the feeling that I am the only one who will protect my heart and look out for me. Because that is not true!! The God and Creator of the universe will protect my heart if I give it to Him. And because of that, I can have victory even now. Even in the midst of the wilderness, there is victory. You, too, can trust that victory is coming, friend.

Looking back, I see the new sprouts with healthy roots that sprung up in my soul. On the most challenging days, I can cling to how far God has brought me. The beauty of the wilderness is that we are not alone. In fact, sometimes, it is where we feel closest to God. He promises us streams in the wilderness!! How beautiful is that? Just as He provided manna and water for the Israelites, He provides streams for us in our wilderness. He doesn't leave us there alone, He always provides, and that might be seemingly the bare minimum. But when the bare minimum is streams from the Lord, you are blessed because they are glorious streams of heavenly water straight from His heart. The streams are His beautiful attributes that make Him a good Father. He reveals His compassion, provision, love, rest, and glory.

I don't know what kind of struggles you are walking through today. But I'm sure that on your journey, something has tested you and left you uncertain about how you would come out of it. My prayer for you is that the story of the Israelites in the wilderness will remind you of God's faithfulness to His children. Let it be an encouragement that even on your darkest day, God has not abandoned you. He plants little streams of His faithfulness in our lives just as He did for the Israelites; we just have to look and be open to them.

We can learn so much from the Israelites. We are the Israelites in many ways. Let us release our plans and ways to Lord so that He might lead us to our Red Sea and display His glory for all to see!

> But he said to me, "My grace is sufficient for you, for my power is perfected in weakness." (2 Corinthians 12:9 CSB)

You probably don't have it all together. You aren't supposed to! The glory is not ours to receive on this earth. The glory is all due to Him, the Almighty Creator of the universe. So, rest in your weakness, surrender your plans, and trust in the Lord; because His power is perfected in our weakness!

I encourage you, friend, to grip on to the Lord during your time of pain and struggle in the wilderness. He is the only thing that stands true and firm. You can trust Him with your whole heart because He will protect you, provide for you, and lead you to the promised land. He will see each of our journeys complete, and it will glorify Him if we surrender our ways.

Whether or not you see the completion of your wilderness season on this earth, remember that He has already won the battle if your heart belongs to Him. So we can face each day, each challenge, and each battle knowing that He has already gone before us, and He is walking with us through the plan that He has made. We might not see the fulfillment until we're in heaven one day, but our souls can be content knowing they belong wholly to Him.

The biggest lesson I've learned so far is that the only thing we are promised is the ultimate satisfying communion with the King of kings, and that comes only when we give our lives to Him. Through our communion with Him, we always have victory, and we will never be lacking. Even in the darkest times. Allowing us to fully embrace each step of our journey.

EMBRACE GOD'S GOODNESS

by Julie T. Jenkins

David, the author of many of the Psalms, embraced and extolled the goodness of God. But David's awareness of God's goodness did not originate from a life of ease! As a young man, he worked as a shepherd, living out among the sheep – sleeping on the ground in the elements and fighting off wild animals. And although he was overlooked as the youngest of Jesse's family, David stood strong against the giant Goliath, invoking the name of the Lord. This brought him into the court of King Saul, who then spent the rest of his life hunting David from a place of jealousy. Yet through it all, David looked past his own suffering and inconveniences and sang and wrote of the goodness of God.

I wonder if David was inherently joyful or if he wrote songs and psalms to remind himself to look for God's goodness. I wonder...because there are days when I have to remember to look for God's goodness...to remind myself...

Our God CREATED the world, and everything in it, for us.

Our God PURSUES us because He loves us.

Our God FORGIVES even the worst of our sins.

Our God GIVES GENEROUSLY to all those who ask.

Our God PROTECTS us from evil and wickedness.

Our God is RIGHTEOUS and JUST.

Our God PROVIDES for all our needs, even when we don't know what we need.

Our God extends MERCY when we are in distress.

Our God is PATIENT and STEADFAST, even when we seek joy in all the wrong places.

Our God is our REFUGE when we are in trouble.

Our God is LOVE, and His love endures forever.

Our God always LISTENS when we call on Him.

The world is not perfect. Trials will come against us. We will sin, and some days will be hard. But there is one thing we can count on – through it all, God's GOODNESS will always remain. That is why David could sing. And that is why we can sing. Every. Single. Day. We can embrace God's goodness, and we can even reflect His goodness.

The next time you have the opportunity to go outside on a clear night, I encourage you to spend some time gazing at the moon. The moon does not give off any light of its own, but even in the darkness of the nighttime sky, it often shines bright enough to light our path. The moon is just a massive chunk of rock, positioned to shine in the dark as it reflects the light of the sun. As children of a GOOD God, you and I are positioned to reflect God's goodness, even when the circumstances around us look bleak and dreary.

So remind yourself! Read the Psalms. Sing worship music. Dance in the rain. Turn your face to see the goodness of God. And in doing so, allow His light to reflect off YOU, for all the world to see!

Elizabeth Anne Bridges

is one of seven children from an Air Force family and has traveled the world, even living in England briefly during the Vietnam war with her British-born mother and grandparents. She has two children and two teenage step-grandchildren. They are each her heart.

A graduate of Pembroke Christian Academy in Pembroke Pines, Florida, Elizabeth received a degree in Business administration from Cumberland University in Lebanon, Tennessee, and has worked extensively in the human resources field for 20 years.

Elizabeth enjoys gathering Christian devotional books for adults and children at the domestic violence center, desiring to introduce them to salvation through Jesus Christ and mentor them to walk daily in obedience to Him. Because of her traumatic past, she can uniquely relate to these individuals. She dearly loves her brothers and sisters in Christ and wants them to have an abundant life free in Jesus Christ.

Additionally, she is a dog lover, an avid bird watcher, and a nature lover. One of her goals is to buy every field guide the Audubon society produces on all things nature.

FINDING MY SAFE PLACE IN CHRIST

by Elizabeth Anne Bridges

The Lord is close to the brokenhearted; he rescues those whose spirits are crushed. The righteous person faces many troubles, but the Lord comes to rescue each time. (Psalm 34:18-19 NLT)

Sometimes I look back on my life and wonder how I survived through it all. But God's grace carried me through the storms. And not just a rain shower but a full tornado or hurricane of my heart and soul. My story is one of abuse and trauma, but although that abuse changed my life forever, it does not define who I am. My abuse and trauma from sexual battery began when I was about 2 or 3. It continued until I was 16. It was not just one offender. It was multiple people, including relatives and strangers. It culminated when I was abused for the last time at the age of 16. When I was trafficked.

But let's begin at the beginning. My father began abusing me when I was 2 or 3 years old. He began fondling me and performing oral sex on me when my mom would leave me with him to take my other three siblings to Brownies or Boy Scouts. I believe my father started abusing me because of a lust he had cultivated while serving in the military in the Korean and Vietnam wars. Young children and women were readily used for prostitution in those countries. There was one point when I was five that I became so raw that I could no longer urinate and was taken to the emergency room bleeding heavily from my bladder. My father oversaw the military police at our base. He told them I had fallen on the monkey bars and the bar had landed between my legs. I guess because of his position nobody gave any thought as to whether that was the truth. I can remember the times that my mom would leave me with him. I would be filled with dread and fear. He would say, "Do not tell mommy or your brothers and sisters. You're my favorite Karen, my poodle." (Poodle was my nickname because my hair was so curly.) I really did not want to displease him. My dad was a severe disciplinarian. He would whip my brothers with a belt - usually with them kneeling in front of him with no shirt on.

The abuse paused while my father served two tours in Vietnam. He came home early because my mom was ill. Within months of him retuning home, my mother died of leukemia. My childhood trauma was not limited to sexual abuse. My siblings and I were scared daily. My father's behavior became very erratic as he started drinking heavily to deal with the grief of my mother's death and the trauma he endured in Vietnam. When I was in first grade, he drank severely and was often passed out when I came home from school. There were times he would ask me to comb his hair. As I did, he sometimes fell asleep and slid from the chair onto the floor. One time I thought he was dead. I grabbed a glass and held it over his mouth to see if it would steam. It did not, so I grabbed a pitcher of water and poured it on him. He woke and stumbled to bed. Days were like that. Very scary and full of fear for me and my brothers and sister. We might go to a favorite pizza restaurant on Fridays and he would become so drunk my brothers had to drive us home at the ages of 13 and 11, barely able to see and reach the pedals to work the car.

The sexual abuse started again as he began to have me sleep with him at night instead of with my sister. He said he wanted to stop us from talking and staying awake all night. The fondling started again and culminated with full intercourse twice. During that same time, he tried to stop drinking and would send us to stay with neighbors and relatives, hoping the break would give him what was needed to get over the grief and trauma he was dealing with. The system tried to step in, my sister and I spent time in foster care after my father had a heart attack. The boys were sent to stay with friends. Once a female school teacher from my brother's school took all four of us siblings home for a weekend. Sadly, that ended up with her fondling me in the shower and taking me into her bed. There were also people who worked with my brothers at a newspaper company who abused me while they were "taking care" of us, forcing me to perform oral sex when I was seven.

Things took a terrible turn for my father after he forced me to have intercourse. He got his service revolver and told the boys he was going to kill himself and me so that we could go see my mom in heaven. The boys took the gun away and removed the bullets. He later drank alcohol and took valium in excess and was taken to the hospital, where he died of a heart attack. I think his wanting to kill me stood in my mind, and I wondered if I was responsible for his death.

One of the most trying times in my life after my parents' death was when a relative who had custody of me at the time decided to traffick me at a heavy equipment show. This relative used me as a prostitute for vendors and attendees. A lot of money was involved as this relative carried two dealerships for one of the major vendors at the show, and each year he hired prostitutes. That year, he could not find a prostitute to hire. He told me to come to the show, that my job would be completing name tags. When I got there, I was led away by four young men. Gagged, blindfolded, and tied so I could not resist. My relative told the men that I was underage (but not that I was his relative), so they were to only have sex with me anally to prevent being charged. I could also be fondled and touched. I was laughed at, taunted, and called a whore and a bitch. Even though I could not answer, they asked me questions like, "Don't you love this whore? Isn't this why you came, you dumb bitch? Why are you crying and fighting? You know you want it."

From the age of 2 until 16, I counted 25 people that sexually abused me. It is mind-boggling to realize how easily and quickly a child can become abused sexually. It takes minutes to happen. When I turned 18, I became an adult in the eyes of the court, which meant I was no longer in the custody of the relative. I was finally free. Although I was physically no longer in harm's way, I had so much healing to do emotionally, spiritually, and even physically. Satan had spoken lies to me. Lies that I kept in the back of my mind. I did not realize that some of my actions sexually with the few boyfriends from high school and eventually my husband were a direct result of what I had inherently been taught through the abuse. I felt that men only wanted women for sexual gratification.

I got married to my husband quickly after I left my relative's home at age 18. We met water skiing with my sister and his sister, who were friends. I strove to please my husband sexually to excess. In joint counseling I once said I was a sex slave. I believed that sex was the only reason my husband loved me. I could not believe anything else after the abuse. But, I was learning that I was not the horrible thoughts that Satan had put in my head. It still took more time and healing.

So Christ has truly set us free. Now make sure that you stay free, and don't get tied up again in slavery to the law. (Galatians 5:1, NLT)

I later told my husband about the abuse, and he was so horrified that he chose not to believe me. I had been diagnosed with multiple sclerosis, a chronic illness affecting the immune system – studies have shown that people who have suffered abuse often have autoimmune diseases. I began taking medicine to prevent the progression of the disease and other medication for symptom management. Unfortunately, these caused suicidal thoughts and anxiety, which, combined with the stress from acknowledging my abuse, led me to three suicide attempts through overdose. My husband and I then separated after 32 years of marriage.

After I left my husband, I dated a man who loved guns. I was still traumatized, and I tried to kill myself with a handgun. But I blew a hole in the wall trying to practice pulling the trigger on a big 45. He took the gun away. I left him after he became abusive.

I attempted suicide one more time with an overdose, but again God saved me. I threw up the medication. I began to realize God loved me and did not want me to die. It was then that my healing began in fervor.

> *My sheep listen to my voice; I know them, and they follow me. I give them eternal life, and they will never perish. No one can snatch them away from me, for my Father has given them to me, and he is more powerful than anyone else. NO one can snatch them from the Father's hand. The Father and I are one.* (John 10:27-30, NLT)

I was now single again, and I began to focus on journaling and writing down the trauma incidents in detail. As I did, God would bring each incident to mind and reveal more and more of the details at the right time. It was always at a perfect time, when I was alone and felt safe. At first, the amount of anger

I felt towards my abusers was incredible. I could not believe the thoughts that I had, wishing severe punishment on those who had hurt me. I truly wanted them to feel the same hurt they had caused me, including the terror and degrading humiliation. Then my journey became trying to understand why it all had happened and why any of those people would use me so selfishly and brutally. How could 15 people choose to rape me and attack me and taunt me at the heavy equipment show? Finally, I began to realize what I had known and heard before: Satan is a liar out to kill and destroy everyone, especially those who trust in God.

> *For it is by believing in your heart that you are made right with God, and it is by openly declaring your faith that you are saved.* (Romans 10:10, NLT)

I accepted Jesus into my heart at age 7. After my parent's death, we went to live with a relative whose wife was a Sunday school teacher. She introduced each of us to Jesus and what He did on the cross. We each accepted Him as Lord and Savior and were baptized.

Throughout my healing process, I had to go back to God's command to forgive others as He has forgiven me. *Make allowances for each other's faults, and forgive anyone who offends you. Remember, the Lord forgave you, so you must forgive others.* (Colossians 3:13, NLT) It was hard initially to look at each incident and say, "I forgive you." I could only do it with the grace of God and by His strength. I remembered Jesus' crucifixion and the suffering He took on Himself as a blood payment for our sins. I had previously watched Mel Gibson's movie *The Passion of the Christ* and remember visually what Jesus incomprehensibly endured for each of us. I forgave each of those men and my family members. Finally, the terror, humiliation, and trauma of those acts began to go away.

Then I took further steps to heal my mind and body. I began to do music therapy. Listening to nature sounds and classical music. Both which are proven to soothe and heal. I joined supportive Christian groups on Facebook. I joined Women World Leaders, read the daily devotions and the free bimonthly magazine and listened to the podcasts. I joined several pastor websites with downloadable podcasts such as Joel Osteen and listened to his uplifting and positive messages. Steve Furtick from Elevation Ministries supplied me with incredible anointing powerful messages. I also joined Dr. Phil to hear of others' suffering. Even though every story he does is not related to sexual abuse, it brought me back to the reality that everyone suffers, and every family suffers and struggles.

The biggest lie that Satan gives you is that you are alone in your pain. That is not true - all people and families suffer. My next step, staying in and memorizing the Word of God, put me on further solid ground. I had been in church most of my life, but I began to attend church and Sunday school or small groups consistently. This took discipline. I made the decision long before church on Sunday that I was going, no matter what. I downloaded a Bible app and began to read the New Testament with my church. I also read devotional plans on every subject. I immersed myself in the Word of God. It is only when you know the truth that your mind and body can become set free.

I also began walking to get the anger and tenseness out of my body. I joined a gym. All the years of fight and flight had been adding cortisol to my body. I began to be silent with God and meditate so He could speak to me. I laid down on the carpet, closed my eyes, and welcomed Him in. I am always face down on the carpet in humility to Him. He would speak as I focused on seeing Him. He gave me words of love, direction, and sometimes discipline. Being alone with God and clearing your mind to hear Him takes diligence. But when you do, you will be richly rewarded with His presence. He longs to spend time with you because He loves you so.

As I relive these events in my life, I have to say that life is NOT over despite any violent actions meant to destroy you. If you lived through the incomprehensible, you are a survivor by the grace of God. That is the first truth in Him that you need to believe. The evil and perpetrators did not win. You did. Nor are you defined by things forced on you during sexual abuse and trafficking. You're not tainted or worthless. You're not meant to fulfill someone's sexual desires against your will. That is not your only value to this world. And it is not your future with someone you love either. You can heal from the trauma.

And you can forgive, by acknowledging that your pain was caused by the willful sin of someone else. They succumbed to the temptation and lies of Satan. They used their own free will to go through with that horrific desire for lust. Satan will stop at nothing to destroy people's lives. Both the victim or the person committing the offense.

The good news is that there is a world filled with good, godly, Spirit-filled people, people who have values and morals that line up with the Bible. Once trust is broken due to trauma, it can be difficult to know who to trust. Measure people as the Bible instructs. *Yes, just as you can identify a tree by its fruit, so you can identify people by their actions.* (Matthew 7:20, NLT) Is that person good, kind, gentle, and empathetic to the needs of others? Do they walk with honesty and integrity? Are they fellowshipping with other believers on a regular basis? Look at yourself and other believers' lives, and pray that you will have these traits in your life.

"FRUITS / of the SPIRIT"

> *But the Holy Spirit produces this kind of fruit in our lives; love, joy, peace, patience, kindness, goodness, faithfulness, gentleness, and self-control. There is no law against these things!* (Galatians 5:22-23, NLT)

Since we are living by the Spirit, let us follow the Spirit's leading in every part of our lives. (Galatians 5:25, NLT)

God is the ultimate Father [Abba Father]. He doles out justice to all His children according to His timetable. He loves, defends, and corrects all His children. We are all one body in Christ, and each of us is a part of that body. And each of us is needed to edify and build up the body. We are here to teach others to know and be more like Him. We can impact this world for His glory and honor by serving others and being a light in a world that can be so dark. When you start living with this knowledge, you can learn to have peace in your soul and mind.

Then you will experience God's peace, which exceeds anything we can understand. His peace will guard your hearts and minds you as you live in Christ Jesus. (Philippians 4:7, NLT)

When all the horrific abuse was going on, my safe place was with my mom. We lived a few blocks from the cemetery where she was buried. In my mind, I would go into the ground in my own safe wooden box next to her coffin. I would sit in my box and hold my hand against it, hoping to feel her through the wall. Knowing that one day I would see her again, I hoped. Knowing that she was the only good thing I had in my life, I hoped. But now I know that I will see her again, with my assurance of salvation and hers. But more importantly, I no longer must stay in that safe place I did as a child. Now I have my safe place in my Lord and Savior Jesus Christ, and my heavenly Father. And in the Holy Spirit that lives inside me to tell me what the Father wants me to do each day. And on some days, remind me of what to do when I am busy. His grace is never-ending. My favorite scripture now is Psalm 91:1-2, *Those who live in the shelter of the Most High will find rest in the shadow of the Almighty.*

This I declare about the Lord He alone is my refuge, my place of safety; he is my God, and I trust him. (NLT) I meditate on my new place of safety daily and read the entire chapter that promises His protection. We are free, dear Sisters of God. We are free with a true, perfect, loving Father all the days of our life. Rest in that. Have peace in that. I love you. And He loves you more and perfectly.

God LOVES you,
We are free with
a true perfect, loving
FATHER!

* ABUSE →

pulling summit →

* Women WORLD leaders →

Google Meet →

Google Meet →

Embrace Grace

by Kimberly Ann Hobbs

Grace is the love of God shown to the unlovely, peace that He gives to those who are restless, and favor toward the unworthy. All throughout Scripture, especially the New Testament, we are shown how God loves His creation, even when they do not deserve it.

How do we embrace His grace? We understand and acknowledge that we have fallen short of living righteously. The Bible tells us:

 For all have sinned and fall short of the glory of God.
(Romans 3:23 NIV)

Because of God's grace, He provided our Savior, Jesus Christ. Once we acknowledge this and accept it for ourselves, we can embrace the kind of grace we should have for others, knowing that all of us are in the same sinful state. We have fallen short of the glory of God. We live in a world of earning, deserving, and merit, and these result in judgment. That is why everyone wants and needs grace. Grace is "mercy, not merit." Grace is getting what you do not deserve and not getting what you do deserve.

As Christ-followers on our path to spiritual growth, we continuously make mistakes because of our sinful nature, and we live every day by the grace of God. The same grace He shows us, we need to show others. Thankfully, through forgiveness according to the riches of God's grace, grace drives our sanctification – our spiritual growth. We strive to train and renounce the ungodliness and passions of this world and learn to live upright and godly lives, helping point others to do the same. Spiritual growth does not happen overnight; it is something we grow in. We "grow in the grace and knowledge of our Lord Jesus Christ." (2 Peter 3:18 NIV) Grace transforms our desires, motivations, and behaviors. God's grace empowers us!

> *This same grace teaches us how to live each day as we turn our backs on ungodliness and indulgent lifestyles, and it equips us to live self-controlled, upright, godly lives in this present age.* (Titus 2:12 TPT)

As recipients of God's grace, we are privileged to serve as agents of grace. When we believe and receive what Christ did on the cross for payment for our sins, we receive God's grace. And the Word of God encourages us to continue in grace (Acts 13:43), testify of God's grace (Acts 20:20), and live with hope beyond death.

God's Word is all about God's grace through Jesus Christ. The apostle Paul even calls it "the gospel of the grace of God." (Acts 20:24 KJV)

> *And just as sin reigned through death, so also this sin-conquering grace will reign as king through righteousness, imparting eternal life through Jesus, our Lord and Messiah!* (Romans 5:21 TPT)

There is an endless fountain of grace that God opened for us in Christ. We are encouraged to embrace this grace, a "gift" to us that is completely free and ours forever!

Grace is actively and continually working in the lives of God's people. Grace is the ongoing, benevolent act of God working in us without which we can do nothing. Grace is given to us to serve others and empower us to exercise our spiritual gifts to build up those God puts in our path.

Because of who God is and all that He wants to accomplish within us, He commands us to extend grace to others. Forgive them, love them and be kind to them, even if they make it extremely hard to justify doing so, and you will grow in such a spiritual way. The grace you show to others will be multiplied back to you. Give grace and see yourselves and others receive the permission to be "God's work" in progress.

. . . .

Deb Hogan

compassionately weaves her vivid life experiences with scriptural principles to assist people in weathering the storms of life. Walk out of Worry ministry was born after Deb discovered that she had inherited a life-threatening illness. She began to write and deliver inspirational speeches for women's conferences. Now, as a devotional writer for Women World Leaders, Deb draws on her journey as a cancer patient. Deb has been married over 30 years to her husband, Mark, and has two adult daughters, Jessie and Grace. Deb recently became a grandmother to Oliver, and she finds this stage of life so fulfilling.

The following verse helps Deb make sense of her suffering. "In the world you WILL have trouble but take heart, I have overcome the world." (NIV John 16:33)

Deb can be contacted at dhogan9297@comcast.net

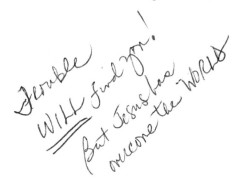

Trouble WILL find you! But Jesus has overcome the WORLD

WALK OUT OF WORRY

by Deb Hogan

The stage was set for a worry-filled life from the beginning. I was born two months early, on Christmas day. Imagine my mother's surprise when she sat down for Christmas dinner and her water broke! I was supposed to be born in February. The Lord decided that I would be born on Christmas day, and I count it a privilege to share His birthday. I was around 2.5 pounds, and I spent the first month of my life in an incubator. My mother had been sick during the pregnancy, and her symptoms persisted after I was born. A CT scan revealed that she had a brain tumor. So while I went to intensive care, my mother went to the operating room for brain surgery. My mother had a hereditary disease called von Hippel-Lindau, or VHL. The disease causes benign and cancerous tumors to grow in the brain, spinal cord, retinas, and kidneys. My mother told me that after I was born she cried as she rocked me, wondering if she would live to see me grow up. She underwent 13 hours of brain surgery, radiation treatments, and long weeks of rehabilitation. So when I was discharged from the hospital, I went to live with my grandparents. This began a series of separation moments that would continue throughout my childhood. The worry cycle began.

My mother recovered, and life returned to normal. My parents lived in a beautiful brick house that my father built in Newton, Massachusetts. We lived next door to my father's childhood home, where he grew up as the baby of 11. My paternal grandparents had immigrated from Italy. Life was difficult for my parents as my mother continued to suffer with tumors and surgeries. When I was 7, my parents divorced. I vividly remember the day we left my dad and that beautiful brick house. Life was again on shaky ground. My foundation was crumbling, setting me up for a life of worry. My mom and I settled in at my grandparent's home. One day my mother decided she needed to "sow her wild oats." She wanted to live on her own and party as she now had VHL and she didn't know how long she would live. So that meant I would be left behind. It is interesting to see how we repeat the patterns of the past. My grandmother had left my mother when she was 11 months old for the same reason, leaving my grandfather to raise her alone. My maternal grandmother would eventually die in her 40's from VHL.

I settled in with my grandparents, who lived in a pretty yellow house on the corner of a busy street in Waltham, Massachusetts. I went to a new school, had a best friend across the street, and another best friend a few houses away. I had a warm bed and grandparents who loved me. My dad visited often. I began to relax and feel safe again. But in the back of my mind, I wondered what my future held and what would happen next. A few years passed, and my mother started to take an interest in me. I was around 11, and she recognized that I could help around the house and do things for her. Her recent back surgery had left her with chronic pain, so you guessed it - my mom asked for me back. My grandparents had no choice but to let me go. So I left my school, my best friends, and that pretty yellow house on the corner of a busy street and went to live with my mom. She worked as a receptionist, but we lived at the poverty level. We needed food stamps to eat and we lived in run-down apartments. One time we were evicted and could not afford a moving van. I remember my bed was on wheels and I had to push it along Main Street to our next apartment. Life was hard, and I was often fearful about my future. "What is going to happen next?" and "What does my future hold?"

One day I came home from school and I found a man inside our front hall. He was standing outside the door to my mother's bedroom. I could hear her talking on the phone. I wasn't too concerned because my mother did date and I thought she knew him. I opened the door and let him in. I sat down on a chair in her bedroom to watch him. Something didn't feel right. I discovered from the expression on my mother's face that she did not know him. She rested the receiver on the bed so that her friend could hear what was going on. I remember watching this man fidget as he stood in front of my mother. The next thing I knew, he pushed my mother against the bed and proceeded to pull up her skirt. He must have forgotten that I was there, and when I screamed, he ran from the apartment. My mother's friend called the police. We got the license plate number, and later he was arrested for attempted rape. Needless to say, I was shaken to the core. "What would happen next?" "What did my future hold?"

My mother had more tumors that required surgery. She was not on speaking terms with my grandparents, so this meant that I would often stay with strangers when my mother was hospitalized. I often wondered if she would come back for me.

When I was 13, my mother married a man 20 years older than her. We moved to another town, and I started junior high in a new school. I started singing in chorus and auditioning for plays. I met some great friends. We lived in a safe neighborhood and had a nice apartment. My mother was less controlling and she finally let me go away for a week with my dad and stepmom. I began to let my guard down. I actually had hope that all would be well. A while into my mother's new marriage, my stepfather and I discovered that my mother was drinking. We would find glasses of whiskey all around the house as if she poured her drinks then forgot about them. My mother had another back operation, and she was let go from her job. She worked at an architectural firm from the age of 17 - she loved that job. This loss and chronic back pain sent her into a depression. She started drinking to numb the pain,

One day I came home from school, and saw my mother's purse but could not find her. I repeatedly called her name. I was starting to get scared as I searched from room to room. The last room I looked in was the bathroom. There she was, lying fully clothed in an empty bathtub. She did not respond when I spoke to her. I was terrified and I ran out of the house, thinking she was dead. I called my stepfather at work and he came home. My mother was alive but had passed out from drinking.

It wasn't long after this that there were signs my mother's marriage was in trouble. She did decide to seek help for her alcoholism and went to rehab. While my mother was gone, my stepfather made plans to move out. One day, he knocked on my bedroom door and said that a moving company would arrive shortly, he planned on divorcing my mother, and would I be so kind as to let her know? I was dumbfounded! Later, I shared this with my poor mother, who was still in rehab. This landed her in the psych ward for three weeks. I went to stay with my dad while uncertainty about the future fueled my feelings of anxiety. "What would happen next?" "What does the future hold?"

My mother did leave the psych ward, and she called my father, wanting me back. I was reluctant, however, because I wanted to live with my dad. I adored him. Yet, I felt a sense of responsibility to help my mother. So, I went back. I changed schools again. And started high school. My mother used to sing a song to me called "You and me Against the World." "You and me against the world. Sometimes it feels like you and me against the world. And for all the times we've cried, I've always felt that God was on our side. And if one of us is gone. And one of us is left to carry on. Then remembering will have to do. Our memories alone with see us through. Think about the days of me and you. You and me against the world." Two days before I graduated from high school, she died.

God was drawing me to Him that year my mother was dying. I felt this need to know God, but I hadn't been raised in a Christian home. I remembered there was a Bible in the house that had my mother's name on it - a gift from completing Sunday school, I think. I turned to the only Scripture I had heard - Psalm 23: "The Lord is my shepherd. I shall not want." I started memorizing Scripture to draw closer to Him. I also started attending a Methodist church down the street from my grandparent's house. I just walked in as a 17-year-old and said, "Teach me about Jesus!" There was a lovely female pastor who helped me through the hard days ahead. This yearning that I felt for the Lord led me to go to a Christian college. I learned that I was a sinner in need of redemption. I asked Jesus to save me from my sin and put me on the right path. He filled me with the Holy Spirit, and I began to serve Him using my musical gifts. I also was asked to be a youth leader. So I sang solos and worked with youth as I grew in faith.

I met my husband Mark while I was in college, and he also committed his life to the Lord and was baptized. My worries took a back seat during this time. I seemed to float on air! I stopped thinking about my fears of getting VHL and subsequently stopped the annual retinal exam designed to find retinal angiomas. I thought that because I was now a Christian, bad things wouldn't happen to me anymore. God knew that I had had enough trials as a child. The rest of my life would be smooth sailing! So I graduated with a biology degree which helped me get accepted into a Physical Therapy program. Mark and I got married. We bought a house and enjoyed being a couple, continually growing in the Lord. I stopped saying, "What was going to happen next?" Or "What did my future hold?" I trusted that God only had "good" for me and that "good" meant no more trials!!!!

Mark and I had two daughters, Jessie and Grace. One Sunday after I led worship at my church, Jessie went to a friend's house and Grace came home with me. Mark was working.

Grace and I settled in, had lunch, and relaxed. The next thing I remember is waking up on the couch. I was groggy and a bit confused. It wasn't like me to take a nap and leave Grace, who was 3-years-old, unsupervised. Shortly after, the phone rang and my friend asked if we wanted her to drive Jessie, who was 6, home from her playdate. I had trouble even remembering where Jessie was. Mark came home from work and could tell something was wrong. I got up from the couch and went into the bathroom. I looked in the mirror and saw these broken blood vessels all over my face and chest. Then I opened my mouth and saw that half of my tongue was bruised. I knew then that I had had a grand mal seizure. Now the worries resurfaced: "What is going to happen next?" "What does my future hold? "Do I have a brain tumor?" "Do I have VHL, the disease that ruined the life of my mother and grandmother?" After a series of MRIs and CT scans, it was revealed that I did indeed have a brain tumor. I also had a spinal cord tumor blocking 2/3rds of my spine and cancer in both kidneys. We talked about brain surgery and the possible removal of both cancer-filled kidneys, as well as dialysis. Things didn't look good. My primary care doctor told my husband that I probably had only six months to live.

I no longer had just worries. I was terrified! I feared that I would die and leave my husband and my daughters. I feared that if I managed to live, I would succumb to drug use or alcoholism and live in constant pain from surgeries. I asked the doctor for a sedative. I took one pill when I opened my eyes in the morning and another to sleep. I was consumed by fear. Mark and I got in touch with the VHL Alliance, and they recommended specialists. We found a doctor who specialized in saving kidneys, and he was able to do two kidney-sparing surgeries to remove the cancer and save my kidneys. I had brain surgery as well. We put the spinal cord surgery off because it was going to be a difficult surgery, and we needed to find a specialist. I took a one-year medical leave from my job as a physical therapist.

I started to have panic attacks - nocturnal panic attacks. I would wake up in the middle of the night as if someone had a gun to my head. I thought I was going to die. These lasted for two years. During that time, I was homeschooling my kids and working 4-8 pm, five days a week. Mark and I said "Hi" and "Bye" in our driveway, switching roles for the evening. During this time, I started to dig deeper into my faith. I realized that I had believed the lie that Christians don't suffer, which led me to doubt God's sovereignty and His plan for me. I think this was the root of my fears. Once I learned that God uses suffering for the good of those He loves, I started to look for the blessings in my trials. I also began memorizing Scripture. My life verse became, "In this world you will have trouble, but take heart, I have overcome the world." (John 16:33 NIV) The panic attacks started to subside. I learned to live with a life-threatening disease, knowing my life might be cut short. I rejoiced in each day, praising God that He was sustaining me and giving me peace.

We lived a new normal. I had several more bouts of kidney cancer, needing a total of five surgeries. And I had another brain tumor that required surgery. That large spinal cord tumor was finally removed, leaving me with nerve damage between my shoulder blades. My skin always felt like it was sunburned. I have that pain to this day. I still dealt with those nagging worries about my future as every year we went "tumor hunting" with 5 MRIs. Waiting for the results was nerve-racking, but I kept God's Word with me and exchanged my fears for His peace.

In 2017, after my annual "tumor hunting" expedition, it was discovered that I had tumors in my liver, more numerous to count. This led to a liver biopsy, which revealed that I had pancreatic cancer that had spread to my liver. Stage 4. It didn't look good. I was 53. The worries tried to rear their ugly head, but because I had done so much work to focus on God's sovereignty, I knew He had a purpose and a plan. This Scripture gave me hope: "....all the days ordained for me were written in your book before one of them came to be."

(Psalm 139:16b NIV) He knows the number of my days. I do not have to fret about how long my life will be; I only need to focus on living each day as it comes, with gratitude. My college buddy and I decided to text each other three blessings from our day, every day. We have been doing this for several years, and it keeps us grateful and hopeful. It changes our perspective.

I have been on various cancer-fighting medicines for the past four years, and I will be on chemotherapy for the rest of my life. There is no cure for my cancer. The pancreatic cancer I have (pancreatic neuroendocrine) is slow-growing, so that is a blessing. God is sustaining me. When people look at me and find out my story, they cannot believe their eyes. I look so healthy. The good news is that this cancer hasn't made me sick yet. That day will come. Until then, I live life to the fullest. I get on planes to visit my daughter Grace and my son-in-law Adam in Las Vegas, and I help to take care of my daughter Jessie's son Oliver, who at this writing is nine months old. My husband Mark and I enjoy movies and taking walks by the sea. I take care of my two elderly Siamese cats, Isabella and Lady Slipper. Life is good. This is my aim: "Since, then, you have been raised with Christ, set your hearts on things above, where Christ is seated at the right hand of God. Set your minds on things above, not on earthly things. For you died, and your life is now hidden with Christ in God. When Christ, who is your life, appears, then you also will appear with Him in glory." (Colossians 3:1-4 NIV)

Even as Christians, we have trials in life. I have mine, and I know you have yours. But as we each embrace our journeys, I encourage you to remember that our God is bigger than any trials we may have, and when we keep Him in view as we walk, He will empower us to walk out of our worry, knowing that He has won the battle.

Journal
Lauren 3/2/22

Live
each day
as it is your last !

Love — Be Loved !

Serve —

Live Like Jesus !

Prepared
To meet God
Everyday —

FAITH
TRANSFORMATION

TRIALS — HEALTH

* Hands and Feet of Jesus !
  Long term illness — Lois
  (used car analogy) (can
  (Temporary + Fleeting Life be)

* WE ARE FINE
  WITH WE are not ! (

* We are all going to die —
  cognizant → God's will → Lois still alive —
  God in Control ! Ambassador for God
  again !!

Inspiration — Influences for Jesus !
Focus on Eternal Deposits

Roman 12:2

EMBRACE PERSEVERANCE

by Julie T. Jenkins

If there is one thing this Christian life requires, it is perseverance! Sometimes we are called to walk through fire that seems to last forever. Other times we are called to work for the Lord, and the project is long and arduous. And, of course, there are the times of waiting, when we must persevere even though we don't understand God's plan.

If you are in a season that requires perseverance, it's natural to think, *God, I've done everything you asked me to; why is this not resolved? Why is this so hard?* Even though I can't provide those answers, I can tell you that you are in good company! Jesus understands. He lived on this earth – and His was not a glamorous or easy life. He understands what it is like to persevere through hurt, rejection, and persecution – all while doing God's will. He knows intimately the courage it takes to follow God obediently while waiting for that seemingly far-off reward.

Jesus lived a sinless life, and yet the turmoil that He endured is worse than you and I can imagine. He hung on the cross and took on the sins of the world. Do you know those feelings of guilt that tear at you when you sin? That sick feeling in the pit of your stomach knowing that you have caused harm to someone? On the cross, Jesus endured those very real feelings multiplied millions of times, all while having the ability to stop His own pain and suffering with a single word. But He persevered. For you. For me. Until death. Not a happy ending. Oh, but it was! His perseverance bought us life and changed the world forever! Out of His finished work came the defeat of death itself!

You and I may not understand the good that will come out of our perseverance, but you'd better believe that God - who works all things together for the good for those who love Him and have been called according to His purpose - has a plan! We can wake up each morning and take each step knowing that God is in control and will use all that we are going through for good. Keep up the good fight! Keep battling, working, singing, and praising.

Embrace Perseverance when you are walking through the fire...

The faithful love of the Lord never ends! His mercies never cease. Great is his faithfulness; his mercies begin afresh each morning. I say to myself, "The Lord is my inheritance; therefore I will hope in him!" (Lamentations 3:22-24 NLT)

Embrace Perseverance when the good seems elusive and far-off...

Look straight ahead, and fix your eyes on what lies before you. Mark out a straight path for your feet; stay on the safe path. Don't get sidetracked; keep your feet from following evil. (Proverbs 4:25-27 NLT)

Embrace Perseverance when you just don't see what God is up to...

I press on to reach the end of the race and receive the heavenly prize for which God, through Christ Jesus, is calling us. (Philippians 3:14 NLT)

Embrace Perseverance! Hold on to God for strength and follow His instructions step by step. He WILL get you through! And it will be glorious!

Kelley Rene

Kelley Rene lives in Panama City, Florida, with her husband and mini Australian Shepherd, Blossom. After thirty-two years of marriage, five children, fifteen moves, two continents, and numerous volunteer and paid jobs, she finally seized the courage to activate her passion: writing. She loves to meet new people and experience new places, often the inspiration for her stories. With a longing to be a conduit of God's love and a catalyst for forgiveness, she quickly adopted *Rescued and Redeemed* as her mantra.

Along with her chapter in *Embrace the Journey,* Kelley has published three novellas, *Saving Sabine, Romanian Runaway, Kamilah,* and is finalizing a fourth to be compiled into an anthology, *Way of the Broken.* When she's not scribbling out fiction, you'll find her crocheting, kayaking, enjoying the beach, or cuddling a good book and cappuccino. Keep up with her at kelleyrene.com.

THE CONDITION OF LOVE

by Kelley Rene

> *Love bears all things, believes all things, hopes all things, endures all things. Love never ends.* (1 Col 13:7-8 AMP)

"When do I get my cell phone back?" Just enough sweetness dripped from my daughter's voice to tempt me into complying. But I resisted the temptation.

Missing curfew had become a recurring theme with Caroline. I'd heard enough excuses. The younger children were watching, and I had a standard to uphold. If I caved, she would learn that begging, pleading, and making empty promises would get her out of restrictions. Whenever we doled out a consequence, we had to follow through.

"When you demonstrate that you understand your phone is for communicating with us. Not just your friends."

"How am I supposed to do that without my phone?" Her volume jumped a few decibels.

I longed for my sweet girl - the one who never talked back. Or yelled. Or slammed doors. Where had she gone?

Two weeks later, a smile eased onto Caroline's face when I pulled the desired cell from my pocket and dropped it into her open palm.

Lord, please help her make good choices.

"Remember to call us if you have an emergency or your plans change."

Her smile waned as she scrolled through the many missed texts.

"Be home no later than eight o'clock tonight."

Frustration clouded her eyes. "I haven't been able to do anything in weeks."

"It's a school night." I folded my arms, bracing for a fight. "What time do you think your curfew should be?" It was paramount that all parties understood the terms of this agreement.

She shrugged.

"Nothing is open after ten o'clock." My fingers pressed my forehead to ease the strain. "Be home by then. Not a minute late. You just got your phone back—I'd hate for you to lose it again."

A pout formed on her lips, but she didn't argue as she took the stairs with less enthusiasm than usual.

Heavenly Father, help her be home on time.

. . . .

The battle of wills continued. When she failed to come home one Wednesday night by 3:30 am, I was losing my mind. I frantically dialed all her friends. It took several calls before I hit the mark.

"Missy, is Caroline there?"

The hesitation in her voice told me what I needed to know.

"Hello?" Caroline's voice was nonchalant.

"You have five minutes to get home before I call the police."

"I'm spending the night at Missy's."

"Not without permission."

I rushed to the window when headlights appeared. A boxing match between fear and fury, each taking jabs at the other, pummeled my chest.

The front door thrust open. Caroline's stone-cold gaze met mine, locking on her target. She pressed her lips together and mounted the stairs two at a time.

I barely made it to my pillow before the tears came. *Heavenly Father . . . please, help?*

. . . .

Our new norm pitted Caroline's will against mine. Chit chat, silly jokes, bonding over our love of coffee—now nonexistent. And a husband who traveled more than he was home.

I thought it couldn't get worse. Until the day I poked my head into her room and found she wasn't there. A note lay on the bed. My heart sank.

You're not bad parents, it read, I just can't live here anymore. I love you, Mom and Dad!

Caroline's sprawling signature filled the remainder of the page. Hearts scattered around her name mocked the gloom that welled within me.

A heavy sigh expressed my husband's disbelief. Every *what-if* I'd ever pondered, every insecurity I'd ever felt, and every ounce of faith I'd ever held onto rushed at me with intensity.

Rejection and anguish spilled onto my pillow and dried on my cheeks as my husband cradled me in our oversized bed. Terror stabbed as thoughts fumbled around in my brain. Nothing connected, nothing made sense. Emptiness churned in my gut and rose like molten lava from the depths of a volcano.

Father God, please keep Caroline safe.

We had to wait two days to file a police report.

"Call us if you find her location." The officer's uniform pressed taut around his belly. His arms dangled at his sides. "We'll send a couple of shirts to pick her up."

Was that it? Just wait, until we passed like strangers on the grocery aisle? Or happened upon her at the mall?

We couldn't search the neighborhoods for her car . . . she didn't have one. Unless we were willing to storm every one of her friends' homes, there was no hope. No one knew where she was. Or so they said.

By Monday morning, she had been gone almost a week.

My husband's embrace lingered when he said goodbye before leaving to serve as the chairman of an event five hours away. "Call me if you hear anything."

I could only nod at him and wave as he drove out of sight.

My pride tasted worse than bile as I dialed the school an hour later. "Can you confirm Caroline is present today?" I held my voice steady.

Papers shifted and rustled. "She isn't."

Releasing my emotion through fits of tears and prayers saved my sanity. On the exterior anyway. Where could Caroline be? What might she be getting into?

That night I lay prostrate, my face saturated, begging God to keep Caroline safe and bring her home.

Teachers marked her absent again on Tuesday.

God, is there anything we can do?

My brother came to mind. He and his wife worked with the youth at their church.

He picked up on the first ring. "This is not your fault."

I didn't believe him. This was 100% my fault.

He immediately offered to open his home to her. But I knew she'd never agree to move to Virginia.

I held my breath Wednesday morning as I waited for the secretary to check Caroline's attendance. *Please, please let her be there.*

"She's here."

My hands trembled as I dialed my husband.

"Call Officer Tilman. I have a replacement. I'll be home by dinner." His voice buzzed with energy.

My thoughts whirled. Pack the car. Do laundry. No, wash the clothes, then pack. She couldn't know we were taking her away. She'd never agree to leave her friends.

The loud crank of the air conditioner in the school office rattled my nerves as I watched through a glass wall. I felt like a con artist breaking a prisoner out of jail. Except the prisoner was my daughter, who didn't want to be sprung. Would she turn and run the other way when she saw me?

Anguish and joy bottled-necked in my throat when she rounded the corridor, chatting with the school liaison like old chums.

Caroline tossed her head back at something he said.

Neither acknowledged me when they entered the office.

My relief hardened into frustration.

The sweet scent of honeysuckle wafted in the air as a police officer escorted Caroline from the building and into the back of her squad car. Her brunette hair slicked into a tight bun at the nape of her neck. She was barely older than Caroline.

Lord, help my sweet girl understand we want the best for her.

Caroline climbed into the passenger seat and slammed the door with the force of an earthquake.

God, what can we do to win her heart?

We were home by the time I mustered the courage to ask, "What did the school liaison say to you in the hallway?"

"He asked how old I was." A tentative grin plastered her face.

That was inappropriate. "Why?" I struggled to remain calm and reel in my mounting emotions. I didn't want to get angry. I wanted her to know I was happy to see she was safe. I wanted to reconnect with her.

The grin morphed into smug satisfaction. "He said if I could hold on one more week until I turned seventeen, the police wouldn't make me go home even if you called them."

Her words sucker punched me in the gut. Why would he give her that advice?

She bounded up the round staircase, her hair spinning like the carousel at a carnival.

Given the chance, she'd be gone again.

When the doorbell rang an hour later, I raced out of my bedroom. She would not get away so easily this time.

Caroline dragged an overstuffed duffel in from the porch.

"Would you like a hand?"

She snatched at the bag. "I don't want your help."

Tears assaulted my eyes as I bit back a retort.

. . . .

All afternoon I scurried around, straightening the house, moving clothes from the laundry into backpacks and quietly tucking them unnoticed into the minivan.

Everything was ready by the time my husband pulled into the garage.

His eyes met mine. "How are you going to get her into the car?"

I hadn't ironed out that particular detail. Caroline had hid away in her bedroom all day, not even coming out for lunch.

It's the eleventh hour, Lord. What's the strategy?

The answer came.

I took a deep breath. "Ask her to go for a walk with you." She wouldn't say no to her dad. "Take her for a stroll through the neighborhood. That'll give a minute to figure out the rest."

When the front door closed behind them, I catapulted into a frenzy. "Who wants ice cream?" We never ate dessert before dinner. But the kids' big sister had returned home. It just might work.

I snatched Caroline's favorite blanket and pillow off her bed and corralled the littles into the van. My heart banged against my rib cage, but there was no time to settle my nerves. The garage door squawked behind us as I maneuvered down the driveway.

The hubs and Caroline were heading toward us when I pressed the window down. "Do y'all want to get ice cream?"

Surprise showed on both their faces. They climbed into the car amidst the excited giggles of younger siblings who were unaware of anything other than the promise of a sweet delight.

It would be hours before we stopped again.

. . . .

"We've already passed McDonald's, Chick-fil-A, and Dairy Queen." The rear mirror provided a clear view of Caroline wrestling with her seatbelt in the back.

She pulled her favorite blanket from its hiding place and held a corner in the air. "Where are we going?" Panic filled her voice. She popped around in the seat to inspect the luggage and backpacks stowed behind her seat. "Where. Are. We. Going?" Each syllable landed like a right hook to my conscience.

I giggled, unable to control the anxiety I'd been stuffing all day. We'd been found out.

Caroline clawed past her siblings toward the side door. "Tell me where we're going. *Now.* Or I'm jumping out of this van."

Child locks made that impossible, and besides, the sliding door wouldn't engage while the vehicle was in motion.

Still, her warp-speed threats infused tension into the small space. Her younger brother and sister wailed. Mass chaos ensued.

"Calm down." I mustered command of my nerves and my voice. "Take your seat. When you get hold of yourself, I'll pull over so we can talk."

She let out a blood-curdling scream, the reaction of a hopeless teen who'd lost all control of her circumstances. Sobs echoed from every direction. Caroline. Liam. Sarah. Mikey.

I fought to maintain my resolve and not join the howling choir.

Did we do the right thing? We need your help, God.

"We're coming up on an exit. Calm down so we can talk."

Her cries subsided as we pulled into a rest area.

The littles went off to the restroom with their dad. I turned to Caroline.

She sat in the front passenger seat. Quiet. Void of emotion. Only her puffy eyes testified to her earlier outburst.

I wanted to take her hands in mine. To connect. The beautiful girl we'd always known must be lurking somewhere below the surface.

"Where are you taking me?" A flash of worry laced the anger in her tone.

I hesitated. "To your uncle's house in Virginia."

She didn't hide her relief. "I thought you enrolled me in a military camp for runaways."

I laughed.

She laughed.

For a moment, I wondered why the need for such extremes. "We love you too much to sit back and watch you misdirect your life." The atmosphere shifted.

I laid out the plan. The rules. Caroline would finish high school. She would be mentored by her aunt and uncle. She would come home when all agreed she was ready.

She swallowed hard and gave a small nod. We chatted until the rest of the family returned to the car.

Caroline remained in the front seat when we eased back onto the highway towards Virginia. Conversation came comfortably, an occasional chuckle added to the mix.

Tears swelled all over again when I noticed her sleeping.

Our universe realigned. For now.

· · · · · · · · · · · · · · · · · · ·

By the weekend, being at my brother's was like any other family visit. A nephew's wedding allowed us to hang out with many we otherwise wouldn't have seen. No one mentioned our family drama or the fact that we'd be leaving our daughter there when we left. No one knew Caroline would not have access to the outside world. That would come in baby steps.

When it was time to head home, the enormity of the occasion hit. In four days, my firstborn would turn seventeen. I wouldn't be celebrating with her. Were we really doing this?

"Will you take her to get a pedicure for her birthday? And buy her a cake?" I tucked four twenties into my sister-in-law's hand, camouflaging my deep disappointment. I should be the one taking Caroline for a girls' day out. Guilt and regret nipped at me.

The long drive home was a solemn one. The next week was tough. And the months that followed.

Caroline flew home six months later, finally the loving girl we remembered her to be. Her return completed our family once more. She tested for her driver's license, satisfied her high school requirements, and volunteered to be the associate coach for Liam's pee-wee soccer team. Tough love had been the solution. *Thank you, God, for getting us through this.*

Getting ready for the end-of-season soccer party, I paused while rounding up Liam's gear and poked my head into Caroline's room. "It's clean in here."

She beamed, visibly pleased. "I have a bunch of stuff to donate." Two over-sized trash bags filled the corner. Folded clothes sat evenly stacked on the bed.

The bare walls raised my brows, but distant shouts snatched my attention. "We can drop them off this weekend."

The soccer party was a flurry of pizza, soda, cupcakes, and commotion as all twelve players vied for the coach's attention. Caroline received hugs, gifts, and her own plaque for being a huge help to the coach as well as a favorite of the players. She snapped selfies with several of the teammates.

"I'm heading out." I piled our plates together and dumped my cell phone into my purse. "Are you going to be ready soon?"

The sky was a deep blue as the moon slid into place, and the sun drifted away. I buckled the littles into their seats and rounded the front of the van. Caroline's expression stopped me at the curb.

"I'm not coming home." Her words were quiet. Almost shy.

"What do you mean?" Controlling the emotion in my voice had become my superpower.

"I'm moving in with Haley."

As if on cue, her old friend sauntered out of the restaurant.

Anger plumed in my stomach. Parents, some of whom knew what my last year had entailed, piled out of the pizza joint, doling out hugs and well wishes. How dare she wait until this moment to ambush me?

The muscles in my throat constricted.

A devil sat on my left shoulder and whispered, "Get mad. Really, really mad!"

An angel on the right whispered, "Unconditional love. That's what she needs."

God, how could she?

I swallowed, pushing all selfishness and pride away and allowing humility to take their place. "Caroline, we've gone to great lengths to show you how much we love you. This is your life." The calm in my voice surprised me. "There's nothing you could ever do to take away our love." I paused, then added one last thought. "There's only one thing I ask."

Her brows peaked.

"Call your dad and tell him yourself. I won't be your go-between anymore."

She nodded and reached out for a hug.

I accepted her embrace. "You're always welcome home. Give me a call or stop by anytime." I climbed into the van without looking back.

"Where's Caroline going?" Liam's timid voice echoed the sorrow I felt.

"She's not coming home with us."

His sobs ricocheted around the vehicle, setting off a chain reaction. This time I didn't hold back. Sadness overtook us once more.

. . . .

"Do you want to meet for coffee?" Caroline sounded happy. Excited.

I hadn't expected her to call so soon, much less want to get together. "Tell me where and when."

That coffee date became a weekly event, acting as a bridge in our relationship. It took us from empty heartache to fulfilling friendship. There were bumps and bruises along the way, but love truly conquered the rebelliousness and frustration our relationship had endured for years.

God heard my pleas for help. He provided a way. He kept our daughter safe.

Today, Caroline is whipping up an iced latte while I put the finishing touches on this chapter. Our bond is stronger than ever. I am blown away by God's grace and faithfulness in our lives.

> *We waited in hope for the Lord. He was our help and our shield. In him our hearts rejoice, for we trusted in his holy name.* (Psalm 33:20-21 NIV)

Prayer Requests

Christy: Prayers Career Decision → Corporate World → Right Decision → GOOD TRANSITION, WISDOM & DIRECTION → RENT not BUY

Lois: → Works for more? Very few options for above? Villa or small house → 2K → per month → GOD DIRECT TO SOMETHING QUICKLY — SABRINA → first week, not functioning properly; Meniere's disease → abdominal pain
* Lois — relief complications, bowel blockage → NURSING SCHOOL →
WORK WORKED w/ NASTY PEOPLE → PUMPING w/ SCRIPTURE — HOLY SPIRIT
BULLY'S →

Cathy: Prayers for WISDOM & DISCERNMENT → FOR someone who had gone locations → TRUTH comes out!
* PEACE → grow government → BAD THINGS magnified
BULLY'S @ WORK; underlying concerns →
ZELENSKY BROADCAST TO congress →
PRAISE = counselor

Cheryl: PRAISE — Enjoying her job — PRAISE @ WORK
SLEEP — IS GOOD!
JOB GOD!

Dierdre — Mia @ — Kiera

Embrace Faith

by Kimberly Ann Hobbs

Do not fear or be dismayed. When the righteous call out to God for help, He hears and rescues them from all their troubles.

> *The eternal God is your refuge, and underneath are the everlasting arms. He will drive out your enemy before you, saying "destroy him!"* (Deuteronomy 33:27 NIV)

We have all faced wavering or tired faith, and when we do, we can become discouraged and fearful. This can happen due to job loss, health problems, or even the death of a loved one, leaving us to wonder if God is there for us. So how do we get through these difficult situations?

The Bible teaches that we, through faith, can find security and hope in God revealed through Jesus Christ. And it is precisely when our faith is struggling that it is time to embrace it even tighter, to continue believing, and turn to the scriptures. Because inspiration, encouragement, and hope are all found in Jesus and in His Word.

God tells us we will endure troubles in this world and face many challenges. That is is evident even in some of the chapters of this book. But, the beauty in these stories and struggles is that God promises that we will have victory in faith through Jesus Christ. There is no doubt about that! We can embrace faith because Jesus Christ HAS overcome the world.

If you are going through a strenuous time of despair or grief or facing uncertainty in any situation, use faith scriptures to lift your spirits. Pray for faith and strength continually. When you are unable to handle a situation, remember God IS able. It is not your physical strength that will accomplish anything; it is your faith and belief in the power of God that moves the mountains. It is the faith that flows from Jesus' saving blood. It is HIS strength alone that will sustain you. But it takes strong faith to believe and stand on this. The following verse is one to repeat over and over as needed.

I can do everything through Him who gives me strength. (Philippians 4:13 NIV)

You can do everything, but you can't do it alone. To embrace faith daily, you must pick up God's Word and read it. None of us can keep it together in difficult or stressful times by merely looking at our closed Bible on our desk or nightstand and not communicating with God. Reading God's Word and having prayer time with Him is vital, and we should do both daily.

Faith then is birthed in a heart that responds to God's anointed utterance of the Anointed One. (Romans 10:17 TPT)

And Without faith living within us it would be impossible to please God. For we come to God in faith knowing that He is real and that He rewards the faith of those who passionately seek Him. (Hebrews 11:6 TPT)

Things in this world will come at you, and you must be prepared to combat them with your faith - faith in what God's Word declares as truth.

> *Faith opened Noah's heart to receive revelation and warnings from God about what was coming, even things that had never been seen. But he stepped out in reverent obedience to God and built an ark that would save him and his family...*" (Hebrews 11:1 TPT)

I want to encourage you that we each must strengthen our faith muscle each day. It will not become strong, nor will we have the pillar of strength we desire unless we work to strengthen it daily. Just as your body needs strength training to build endurance to fight off diseases or weakness, so does our faith. Embrace faith with the understanding that God is the One who will navigate you through your circumstances as you look to Him with faith. We build up our power to combat troubles through Him.

> *Trust in the Lord completely, and do not rely on your own opinions. With all your heart rely on Him to guide you, and He will lead you in every decision you make. Become intimate with Him in whatever you do, and He will lead you wherever you go.* (Proverbs 3:5-6 TPT)

This verse so wonderfully displays ultimate faith. Embrace it in its entirety. Hold onto your faith and trust God at every twist and turn of your lifetime. Do not allow your faith to waver. Stay strong and take on every aspect of faith described in God's Word.

Now faith brings our hopes into reality and becomes the foundation needed to acquire the things we long for. It is all the evidence required to prove what is still unseen. (Hebrews 11:1 TPT)

When we develop our faith muscle to become strong, we can experience peace and put away all worry, fear, anxiety, sadness, and depression, having faith in God as our conquerer.

Surrender your anxiety! Be silent and stop your striving, and you will see that I am God. I am the God above all nations, and I will be exalted throughout the whole earth. Here He stands! The commander! The mighty Lord of Angel armies is on our side! The God of Jacob fights for us! (Psalm 46:10-11 TPT)

Embrace faith - pause in His presence and simply trust Him with everything in you.

. . . .

Dr. Chidi Kalu

is the Founder of The Women of Distinction Organization. With a strong cutting-edge word, she ministers powerfully to secular and non-secular environments as a prolific Speaker, published Author, certified Empowerment Life Coach, Corporate Trainer and Management Consultant. She is one of the leaders with Women World Leaders and committed to the ministry of the Gospel. Dr. Kalu has a passion to see all of God's children live a fulfilling life centered on Jesus Christ. She has a master's degree in Administration and a doctorate in Christian Education. For over 25 years, Dr. Kalu has experienced significant impact as the hand of God moves in the lives of those she touches with her prophetic gift of encouragement, teaching, coaching and intercessory prayer. She lives in Alpharetta Georgia and enjoys spending time with her 4 adult children and 3 grandkids.

THERE IS GOLD IN THE FIRE

by Dr. Chidi Kalu

At age 15, I came to the United States from Africa to attend college and immediately plugged into a local church in Northfield, Minnesota, my college town. I went on mission trips within the United States and was honored to share the love of God. In every ministry I was involved with, I gravitated towards prayer and intercession. Doors began opening for me to speak to women and coach them through the life events they faced. I was serving God, a position the devil wasn't happy with, and he didn't hesitate to toss me into the fire. Although I was familiar with the devil's tactics, I did not expect the heat to be so extreme.

When I was 17 years old and in college, I met my future husband, and we got married shortly after. The Lord blessed us with four wonderful children. Life seemed to be great! We were an upper-middle-class family living in the suburbs: we had great jobs and traveled all over the world for businesses. In 2005, after 19 years of marriage and 26 years with the man whom I felt was the love of my life, my world came crashing down when my husband asked for a divorce.

I was one of those ladies who never believed in divorce; after all, I was a praying woman, a director of intercessory prayer at my church for over 20 years. How could this be? I spoke to women all over the world about holding on and trusting God in hard times, yet I couldn't save my own marriage. And I was not even sure when it all broke down. The reason my husband gave for the divorce was that I was too "spiritual." My heart was broken to pieces, and a million questions were running through my mind: *Lord, what about my children's wellbeing? Where do I go from here? What will my friends say? How can I continue encouraging and empowering other women? Was it wrong to serve you, Lord?*

Every effort to make amends with my ex-husband failed. We were at a point of no return. While I was at church on Easter morning, my now ex-husband cleaned out the entire home we built together and took every piece of property, including all four of our children. I lost everything: my marriage, children, home, property, cars, my joy, dignity, business, and income. All gone. I came back to an empty home with changed locks and began one of the loneliest, darkest, most gruesome, heartbreaking, and painful journeys of my life. I went from having it all one day to waking up to homelessness, no transportation, and no money in the bank the next day. I looked up to the sky and wailed the loudest wail ever as I uttered the words, "My God, my Father, why?" I was immediately filled with shame, guilt, despair, sadness, and regrets, and I was utterly confused about how and what had happened. I worried for my children, and I couldn't make sense of what was happening or my family's communication breakdown. For the next 16 years, God took me on a journey unlike any I had ever been before.

A few weeks after my divorce was finalized, my ex remarried, and I was left with $700,000 worth of debt. I went through every emotion under the sun, asking, *was I was not good enough? What was wrong with me? What did I do wrong?* I went through more shame, despair, guilt, loneliness, and feelings of rejection. How was I going to take care of four young children with no child support? I attempted to hold on to the only business I had left, but that had to be dissolved. After several days of tears and having no one to turn to and nowhere to run to, it dawned on me that I was in a deserted place, a place I eventually recognized as my wilderness. Webster Dictionary defines a "wilderness" as, "a tract or region uncultivated and uninhabited by human beings: an area essentially undisturbed by human activity together with its naturally developed life community." Of course, while I was not literally in a wilderness, my experience was metaphorically one, meaning I was in a lonely, unpleasant, deserted place where nothing was flourishing. I felt completely isolated and void of life.

Overwhelmed with grief, shock, heartbreak, and uncertainty, I had a nervous breakdown and ended up in the hospital. I thought for sure my life was not only spiraling downward, but it was about to be over. I held on to the only thing I knew, and that was prayer. Could it be that the Lord had been preparing me from childhood by giving me a love for prayer because He knew I would need to rely on prayer for my wilderness experience years later? He is an all-knowing God, and I thank God that He never left me nor forsook me even when I lost friends and family members whom I thought would stand by me.

After being released from the hospital, I went back to living in my business office - until I lost that. Then I lived with strangers who took me in. I got bounced from place to place as those who offered to take me in could only keep me for a couple of weeks. In this wilderness, I felt alone, tired, dejected, and isolated. It was like being a prisoner in solitary confinement, except that I had permission to leave, but then where would I go?

Does this story sound familiar to you? Despite my confusion, God reminded me of Matthew 4, when the Holy Spirit led Jesus into the wilderness to be tested by the devil. Meditating on the story from the Bible gave me some peace, knowing that if Jesus experienced a wilderness season for some time and got through it, there was hope that God would get me through my circumstance as well.

I never prayed as hard as I did during this season, and I thought to myself, *I wonder if God hears me.* One morning as I was reading my Bible with tears running down my face, I cried out to God, asking him to please reunite me with my children. Suddenly, my eyes fell on Proverbs 3:5-6 (NIV) "Trust in the Lord with all your heart and lean not on your own understanding; in all your ways submit to him, and he will make all your paths straight."

I began learning to dig deeper into the Word of God, and, having nothing or no one else to lean on, my Heavenly Father became my everything. He assured me that although I had lost everything, there was one thing I never lost - His Word. His Word became my necessary food as I drew comfort from it, and prayer became my blanket.

In my wilderness season, I felt cornered with no way out except to give all my attention to the Lord. I was frantically searching for a job as door after door slammed in my face. My days of frustration began to grow as I could not make any sense of all that I was facing. Yet God remained faithful and true to sustain me regardless of my efforts to make it on my own. Finally, after months and months of trying to get back up and hitting roadblocks, I came to a place of surrender, I mean total surrender to God. I had just finished a prayer asking God to please help me, and I surrendered to Him completely. I asked God to take whatever was left of my life and do whatever He chose to do with it. Now looking back, I realize that God often calls us to that place of total surrender where we give up striving in our own strength and yield to all that He has planned for us. After all, His Word says in Jeremiah 29:11 (NIV): "For I know the plans I have for you,' declares the Lord, 'plans to prosper you and not to harm you, plans to give you hope and a future.'"

I began meditating on the promise in Jeremiah 29:11, and although it took me a while, I finally came to terms with the fact that God did have a great plan for my life, even while I was in the wilderness. As terrible as I felt this experience was, it was not meant to harm me but to give me hope and a future. Still, I was in such a low place that I could not see how I would come out of it. Maybe you've been there.

I tried several times to reach out to my ex-husband concerning the children but to no avail. Since I was not allowed to come to their new property, and my children could not come to me, there was no way to see them. My heart longed for them so much, and I would stay up hours into the night wondering if I would ever see them again. Then one day, the Lord heard my prayer, and I got a phone call from my mother saying she would help me get a place to live. As I leaped for joy, we began the process of securing a home. Miraculously, God placed me in a townhome within 30 days. My mother also loaned me her car, and I could see the light at the end of the tunnel.

And as soon as I closed on my home, I got another phone call, one that I had been praying to get for months. My ex-husband asked me to come to get the kids as he no longer wanted them to live with him. This was great news to my soul, and I immediately rushed to go pick them up. Unfortunately, it did not go as smoothly as I hoped it would, but God, in His grace, did get the children to me. We began the painful journey of trying to put our lives back together. It was so tough getting them through high school with one obstacle after another. With little to no income, it was so difficult even to make sure we were all fed. I remember my mom chipping in several times with her limited income as a retired midwife. We held on to our faith in God and the promise He gave me to trust Him and lean not on my own understanding.

During my prayer sessions, I would cry and cry, asking God how He would direct my path, saying, "You said you would make my paths straight, but all

I see are crooked paths, Lord." Not long after, about a year after moving into the new home, I lost that too. My mother's car that I had been using broke down, and the business where I had finally secured a job began downsizing, and I was affected. I was back to nothing again, wondering where I could go now with four children and no money.

Slowly but surely, while still in the wilderness, God began teaching me the importance of abiding in Him. I was reading through the four gospels - Matthew, Mark, Luke, and John – and I decided to stay on John a bit longer. It was then that I gazed upon a scripture I knew so well and marveled as God shed new light on it. Never before had John 15:5 (NIV) meant so much to me: "I am the vine; you are the branches. If you remain in me and I in you, you will bear much fruit; apart from me you can do nothing." I read it over and over and over again while pondering it. I saw that other Bible versions use the word "abide" instead of "remain," and I asked the Lord what He meant. What did He want to say to me? Was this the teaching He had for me in my wilderness? The only answer I received at that time was to go back to His Word and study the lives of others who had gone through a wilderness experience.

Sometimes God does not just dish out answers to us but has us go through the pruning process so that we can truly come out stronger and more fruitful while abiding in Him. I began with Jesus' test in the wilderness that God had already reminded me of. God used the wilderness to prepare Jesus for public service, which would eventually deliver us from our sins and reconcile us to God the Father. I looked up the story of Moses and how, when he was in the wilderness, God prepared him to go back to deliver his people, the Israelites. Elizabeth, Hannah, Ruth, and Sarah all went through their own wilderness experiences when their lives were barren and seemed empty. When there was no fruit and everything was at a standstill, God moved mightily to turn their deserts into places that bloomed and flourished.

As I studied the Bible and made note of these men and women and the great ordeals they faced, I learned three things:

1. They each paid a price and had to yield their lives completely to God, but they were all delivered.

2. They held on to their faith in God, trusting Him even in the most difficult moments until they saw what they were believing for come to pass.

3. God brought them out in His time, not theirs.

As I studied, it began to make sense to me why I had to go through my wilderness season. It is a journey we all take at one point or another in our lives, even though each wilderness experience may come about for various reasons, and the trials and encounters may be different. The common thread is that as we hold close to God in each wilderness experience, in the end, God gets the glory as He accomplishes His plans and purposes.

It has now been 16 years since I got divorced, and I was in the wilderness for 13 of those years. I thought I was in the fire all along, but it only seemed to get hotter and hotter. Through those years, I had to face one trial after another, and each time the heat intensified. And each time the heat turned up, I would hear the voice of the Lord in Job 23:10 (NIV): "But he knows the way that I take; when he has tested me, I will come forth as gold."

The Lord taught me true forgiveness and authentic praise, even when I had tears running down my face. I learned how to remain in Him with total dependency on Him as my provider.

On those days when things were so tough that I did not think I could go another day, the Holy Spirit became my greatest comforter. I would hear

Him whisper the words in 1 Peter 1:7 (NIV): "These have come so that the proven genuineness of your faith - of greater worth than gold, which perishes even though refined by fire - may result in praise, glory and honor when Jesus Christ is revealed."

One thing God assured me was that I would laugh and live again, and this scripture came alive in me through those wilderness years. Romans 8:18 (NIV): "I consider that our present sufferings are not worth comparing with the Glory that will be revealed in us."

What I faced the last few years could never be compared to the glory revealed after the wilderness. I look back at those years when nothing seemed to work out, and I experienced one loss after another, and I thank God that He brought me out. And I thank God that He promises to do the same for everyone who puts their trust in Him. As you remain in Him, abiding and trusting in His Word, He will never fail you. He always brings us out to a place of abundance, just like He said in Psalm 66:12 (NIV): "You let people ride over our heads; we went through fire and water, but you brought us to a place of abundance."

Whatever journey God has us on, we must remember that He is with us always and that He will surely direct that path.

God is faithful. Today as I reflect on my wilderness experience, I can see how the hand of the Lord was on and with me day by day as He led me, taught me, molded me, stretched me, healed me, and then began to restore me. Thank God for the Word of God, such as Isaiah 61:7 (NIV): "Instead of your shame you will receive a double portion, and instead of disgrace you will rejoice in your inheritance. And so, you will inherit a double portion in your land, and everlasting joy will be yours."

Our faithful God has indeed given me a twofold recompense for my former shame, a double portion for all my trouble, and everlasting joy. He is still restoring me as I continue to see Him use those painful moments to develop my faith and prayer life and as He uses my walk and trust in Him as a blessing to others. He has taught me how to be more compassionate and patient and to walk in greater humility and love. He gave me a heart for women who have walked through some of the most difficult and traumatic situations. He wiped away all of my humongous debt, got all four of my children through private college, provided for me to open up a new business, and gave me job opportunities when I needed them. I thank God for my journey to discovery and recovery.

The most important thing that God taught me in my wilderness is one that I hope you will take away from my story: God showed me the blessing that comes when we yield our lives in complete surrender to Him. This is a lesson that I wouldn't trade for anything in the world. Our God reigns. He gives beauty for ashes and He gives gold in the fire. Glory to His Holy Name.

EMBRACE PEACE

by Julie T. Jenkins

What comes to mind when you think of peace? Maybe a quiet mountain stream, a beautiful garden, or, if you are a mom of young children, perhaps a day when the kids are visiting grandma! Peace is the absence of strife, anxiety, and worry, allowing a calm and tranquil heart.

I once heard a story about artists who were challenged to paint a depiction of peace. The winning painting was actually of a ferocious storm! The sky was full of lightning and dark clouds, and the wind was obviously wreaking havoc on the landscape. But in the middle of the storm, on a tree branch, sat a mama bird on her nest. Undisturbed. Experiencing peace in the middle of a storm.

Perhaps that is the kind of peace God has for us in today's chaotic world.

Jesus warned us of this as reported in the gospel of John when He said,

> *I have told you these things, so that in me you may have peace. In this world you will have trouble. But take heart! I have overcome the world.* (John 16:33 NIV)

It is a fallacy to believe that when we come to Christ, God will calm all our storms. When we give our lives to Christ, He does not pluck us out of our messes or the mess of the world. Instead, He surrounds us with His peace even as the walls are falling down around us. And when we feel the flutter of anxiety or stress, as we will, He calls us to pray and rest in His protection, provision, and comfort.

Do not be anxious about anything, but in every situation, by prayer and thanksgiving, present your requests to God. And the peace of God, which transcends all understanding, will guard your hearts and your minds in Christ Jesus. (Philippians 4:6-7 NIV)

As recipients of God's peace, we are also in the privileged position to share God's peace with others. Paul wrote this instruction to the Romans, *If it is possible, as far as it depends on you, live at peace with everyone.* (Romans 12:18 NIV) I love the frankness of the Bible! Simply put, we are to do what we can do to usher in peace, but that doesn't mean that we can always be the peacemakers! After all, we live in a sinful world, and we cannot control others' responses to us, whether it be their response to the Gospel or their response to our input to a situation.

Have you ever been in a circumstance where you were trying your best to handle a situation, but it still blew up? After you have finished praying - asking God how to best deal with the situation - and doing your best to follow His Word and the Holy Spirit's guidance, then it's time to cut yourself some slack. The very fact that the Bible says, *If it is possible, as far as it depends on you, live at peace with everyone, tells us that peace is not always going to depend on us. That's okay. We can trust that God is in control. Our job is to not be overcome by evil, but to overcome evil with good.* (Romans 12:21 NIV)

Besides salvation, I think peace may be the best gift that Jesus granted us. Although God will not necessarily calm our storms, He will, if we let Him, calm our hearts as we walk through the storm. That may even make a day when the kids are NOT visiting grandma fun!

Cindy Jacob Southworth

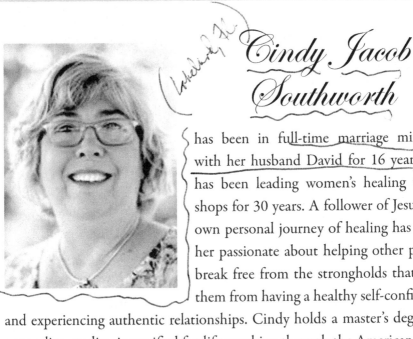

has been in full-time marriage ministry with her husband David for 16 years and has been leading women's healing workshops for 30 years. A follower of Jesus, her own personal journey of healing has made her passionate about helping other people break free from the strongholds that keep them from having a healthy self-confidence and experiencing authentic relationships. Cindy holds a master's degree in counseling studies, is certified for life coaching through the American Assn. of Christian Counselors. She is a John Maxwell speaker, trainer, and coach, a contributing writer for the *Voice of Truth,* and serves on the Leadership Team for Women World Leaders, a ministry that empowers women around the globe. She and her husband are the founders of Breakwater Ministries, and they reside in central Florida. They are the proud grandparents of nine grandchildren.

TRUST THE JOURNEY

by Cindy Jacob Southworth

There's a mass in your bladder. The urgent care physician spoke these words shortly after running a few tests.

I thought I had an acute urinary tract infection, so to say I was unprepared is an understatement. Panic surged through my body. My heart was pounding, my ears were ringing, and I felt like I could possibly have a heart attack. My husband's face was white as a ghost, and he was grasping for the right words to comfort me. I called one of my dear prayer warriors, and she prayed for divine healing. I wanted to call my children, but the phone battery was at 2%. God spoke to my heart: "You need to put that phone down and dial me in right now because your life is about to change." I grabbed my husband's hand, and together we prayed for supernatural strength to face this impending mountain. I was about to embrace a brand new journey of faith.

2017 had been a very stressful year. My father had been placed in a memory care unit due to his progressing dementia, and I was visiting him every other day while juggling our schedule around an active marriage ministry and a growing number of grandchildren. We needed more space for our growing ministry but were having difficulty selling our current home. The necessary surgery was going to be a distraction.

Two weeks after the surgery, the doctor informed me the mass had been aggressive cancer, but he had successfully removed it. He said I would need quarterly checkups for the next year to ensure there were no recurrences. I thanked God for answered prayers and proceeded to the next hurdle of purchasing a home for the ministry.

Three months later, another cancer was removed from my bladder, and once again, the doctor assured me that he got it all, and he would see me again in three months. This time, however, I was not healing as I had the first time. The ministry continued to grow, and the more I contributed to it, the less I focused on my health. My father was moved to a memory care unit closer to my brother, three hours away, which freed up some personal time.

At my next checkup, the doctor started talking about more aggressive measures. As I left his office, I knew I would not see him again because I had lost faith in him. I took these concerns to my Heavenly Father, and He started bringing people into my life who would speak life over me and help me make different choices. I embraced a journey of trusting Him for my next move.

Trust in the Lord with all your heart and lean not on your own understanding; in all your ways submit to him, and he will make your paths straight. (Proverbs 3:5-6 NIV)

Before cancer, I did what I wanted to do. My husband's retirement income supported our life choices, so we had the luxury of working at our own pace. We were very passionate about our marriage ministry, and we worked a lot by choice. It is very rewarding to witness the Holy Spirit's healing of marriages. I enjoyed my time with our grandchildren and other rich relationships in our lives. My life was very full, and while sometimes hectic, it was a life that brought me tremendous joy and strength.

But now, I still had bladder cancer, and no faith in my doctor. Now I was required to put my health first, and everyone else had to take a back seat. I might have cancer, but I was determined that cancer was not going to have me.

> *The Sovereign Lord is my strength; he makes my feet like the feet of a deer, he enables me to tread on the heights.* (Habakkuk 3:19 NIV)

Years ago, I read *Hinds' Feet on High Places* by Hannah Houmard. She shares in this beautiful allegory that our sufferings are glorious opportunities for us to react in a way that reflects God's character. Sometimes we go into the valley before we reach the height of victory, but God will be with us every step of the way.

The first valley I had to overcome was denial; I had to embrace the fact that I still had cancer. The next valley was feeling the loneliness that comes with cancer. Instead of feeling like no one understood, I had to look for people who truly did understand and let them help me. One does not ever embrace a journey like this alone, and I am forever grateful for the people God sent who helped me with the upcoming decisions.

My friend, who is a naturopath, came for a visit. She is as passionate about good health and living a life free of toxicity as I am about great marriages, and we share our love for God. We had rich conversations about our passions, as well as rewarding times of prayer together. She shared a volume of information with me about what I could do to reclaim my health, but frankly, I was overwhelmed. Nonetheless, God was putting me on a path, and she raised awareness of the changes I needed to make.

Next, some dear friends called to pray with me and offered information about Cancer Treatment Centers of America (CTCA). These friends opened doors for me to consult with the brilliant surgeons there. My husband and I made plans to travel to Atlanta.

The weekend before our trip, my father fell and was admitted to the hospital with a broken hip and a brain bleed. Due to his failing condition, the doctors recommended hospice care. The prognosis was grim, and we had to acknowledge that we would be saying goodbye to Daddy within a couple of weeks.

What should I do? My dad was three hours away. I was having symptoms that didn't allow for a lot of traveling. If I were to make the trip to see him, I would have to cancel my trip to Atlanta. I had to make one of the most heart-wrenching decisions of my life and trust my Heavenly Father to give me peace.

 You will keep in perfect peace all who trust in you, all whose thoughts are fixed on you! (Isaiah 26:3, NLT)

I went to my Heavenly Father, and I also visualized sitting with my earthly father. My dad always believed in me and in our marriage ministry. I believed that my work was not yet done on this earth and that I would need to get healthy to keep doing what the Lord had called me to do. My dad knew his own work was finished. I believed with all my heart that my dad would have told me to go to Atlanta, so I did, crying all the way. I knew I would never see my father again this side of heaven, but I went knowing I would have his blessing. The doctor confirmed a week later that I had made the right choice.

I received a call at midnight, May 25, 2018, the night before my surgery. My father had passed away. For the next three hours, all I could do was praise

God. The tears were flowing, and I was dancing around the hotel room, thanking God that my father was no longer tormented by dementia or pain, and he was free to be with Jesus. It was a surreal experience as I pictured my father in the grandstands of heaven, cheering for his baby daughter, who still had work to do here on earth for her Heavenly Father.

The anesthesiologist came in to see me prior to surgery and asked me if I was ready. I shared with him that my father had died the night before. Tears welled up in his eyes, and he said, "And you're here?" I said, "This is where my daddy would want me to be because I'm going to be healed today." They wheeled me into surgery, where I would face my next mountain.

After the operation, the surgeon spoke with my husband. He said there was no evidence of the previous surgeries, and he had attempted to remove a very large tumor but wasn't hopeful that I could keep my bladder. He said he would follow up with a pathology report in a couple of days, and he sent me back to the hotel with a catheter and a very brave husband.

We decided that report would not sway us, and we claimed every Scripture on healing. We called every prayer warrior we knew. I continued to picture my daddy cheering me on, and four days later, the surgeon called and said the pathology report was not as bad as he expected, and he thought he could finish the extraction with another surgery.

One week later, the doctor visited me in the post-op room and gave me a very hopeful prognosis. God was winning this battle for me.

I had a brilliant doctor at CTCA, and I am forever grateful for his skilled surgeries, but it was inconclusive as to whether the cancer was truly gone. He said the logical next step was to remove the bladder to make sure cancer didn't return. I couldn't help but ask what we would do if cancer came back somewhere else. Unfortunately, he couldn't answer that question as he specialized in urology.

I continued to embrace the journey through counsel and prayer.

It's one thing to have tonsils, wisdom teeth, uterus, and even my gall bladder removed, but now I was being advised to have my bladder removed. Not having a bladder would change my daily life significantly, which was confirmed by my dear friend, Jessica, whose bladder had been removed. Her advice to me was, "If I knew there was another option, I would take it." I was desperately looking for other options.

I focused my strength on two areas: my faith and my belief that God created the body to heal itself, and I looked for people who would support these beliefs. I have many faith-filled friends, and they rallied around me with prayer, laying on of hands, anointing me with oil, and sending me Scriptures to support my faith. It became a daily routine for me to stand on the belief that God was healing me. I'm not sure how anyone could do this without a community, and I thank God every day for believing friends who loved me and supported me through these difficult days.

The next hurdle was finding a doctor who believes that the body heals itself. I searched for a doctor who looked beyond the cancer in my bladder. I wanted a doctor who would tell me how I could stop cancer from spreading to other areas of my body. The research ultimately led me to find a doctor with alternative methods, and he was only 60 miles from me.

Now that I had found a doctor who confirmed that my compromised immune system was, in fact, "killing me slowly" and who offered methods for rebuilding my immune system, I had to make some tough decisions. I consulted with his team, and it became clear this was the path I wanted to take, albeit there were no guarantees.

The medical support team said, "This will be your full-time job right now." It was going to require me to take care of myself in a way that was foreign to me. I was used to taking care of everyone else. It seemed selfish and risky as we would have to pay out-of-pocket because our health care coverage only approved conventional treatments. Nevertheless, we spent our life savings, cleared our calendar, learned how to say NO to everyone else, and I said YES to me. I am forever thankful for the doctor who spoke health over sickness, who believes God created our bodies to heal themselves.

My greatest hero was my husband, David. Together, we traveled 120 miles daily for the treatments, which lasted for 5-7 hours. David drove while I rested. That's another thing I had to surrender - I had to trust God to take care of my husband's driving, despite the fact I wanted to sleep with "one eye open" because I felt the need to co-pilot! Part of my husband's role was preparing our breakfast and packing our lunch daily while I packed my supplements. We did this four days a week for twelve weeks, often continuing our marriage ministry on the weekends because I needed to remember my purpose, which helped me believe I was truly going to get well! David took care of me spiritually, as well. He found healing Scriptures and prayed them over me every single night before I went to sleep:

I shall not die, but I shall live, and recount the deeds of the Lord. (Psalm 118:17 ESV)

Then shall your light break forth like the dawn, and your healing shall spring up speedily. (Isaiah 58:8 ESV)

The Lord has declared that He will restore me to health and heal my wounds. (Jeremiah 30:17 NIV)

I pray that I may enjoy good health and that all may go well with me, even as my soul is getting along well. (3 John 2 NIV)

I would love to tell you that my faith never wavered, but that wouldn't be the truth. I grew weary of the treatments. There were days when my body was shedding the toxicity that had built up and caused flu-like symptoms. There were days when my body purged the toxins in me, and I felt like giving up. I would ask my husband if I was going to live, and he said, "Yes, Sweetheart, you are going to live." One night I guess I had asked one too many times, and he looked me in the eyes with so much love and said, "Yes, Sweetheart, you are going to live, but I need you to believe it." I determined then that I would not let the enemy have a foothold in my thoughts, and I began declaring with all my heart that I would be healed.

Though one may be overpowered, two can defend themselves. A cord of three strands is not quickly broken. (Ecc. 4:12 NIV)

Three months later, we returned to Atlanta for a checkup. Although the doctor expected my body to be a complete mess, he was shocked to discover no cancer in my body! My husband and I cried as he showed us a picture of a pink bladder on the screen and no evidence of recurring cancer. I continued quarterly visits, and it took the doctor a year to admit that he had indeed witnessed a miracle. God had restored my bladder to its original state.

The journey continued – in March 2020, another cancer was removed from my bladder. At this time the doctor recommended Bacillus Calmette-Guerin (BCG) treatments, which is a form of immunotherapy. My naturopathic doctor confirmed that this would be the best protocol. However, due to the Covid-19 pandemic, he recommended I find a local doctor to provide the treatments rather than continuing travel to Atlanta. Once again, my faith was tested. And now, due to the lockdown, I did not have the same community I had had before.

The loneliness crept in, and the enemy was having a field day with my thoughts. My faith was being tested - I couldn't understand why this had happened. During the next few months I lost four very close friends, two due to Covid-related symptoms and two to cancer. Jessica's passing hit me the hardest because she had helped me so much on my journey. I couldn't understand why this beautiful young mom had to leave us so early.

"God whispers to us in our pleasures, speaks to us in our conscience, but shouts in our pains; it is his megaphone to rouse a deaf world." C.S. Lewis, The Problem of Pain (1940)

Jessica had embraced life with so much passion, God's love and faithfulness, and a belief that God was going to heal her. He did grant her the ultimate healing when she was ushered into heaven. I realized that I had spent so much time overcoming the fear of the unknown, when all along God was asking me to embrace Him through the unknown. He was shouting for me to choose Him - I had to allow His perfect love to drive out the fear. When we understand that our Heavenly Father is truly in charge of our lives, that we are embracing this journey together with Him, and that He will be with us this side of heaven as well as the other side of heaven, the fear is replaced with an unspeakable joy, allowing us to embrace this side of heaven in a different way.

On my last visit to the urologist, he told me that my bladder looks so good he can't even see signs of the multiple surgeries of the past. Only God can heal scar tissue!

We are all on a journey. The journey becomes sweeter as we embrace the love and compassion that our dear Savior came to give us. He is an all-encompassing Father who delights in us. He will never leave us or forsake us. He will always be here to provide what we need, open the doors that need to be opened, send the right people to us, and protect us every step of the way. When the time comes, He will be there to receive us with open arms and an incredible love that will be so inviting that we won't want to stay here another day. Until that day comes, I will embrace each step of this present journey with His all-encompassing love.

EMBRACE WISDOM

by Kimberly Ann Hobbs

I am sure many of us can say we know someone who is incredibly wise. If you are like me, you gravitate toward wise people. I do because I love to learn from them. On my journey of life, I have noticed there are two types of wisdom - the wisdom of the world and the wisdom that God talks about in His Word. One could say wisdom is the appropriate application of knowledge, and that is so, but God describes wisdom in the Bible as invaluable and its virtue as deep, immeasurable, priceless, and rare. This is the wisdom I wished to attain because I realized, after countless mistakes, that I did not possess the wisdom of God.

I set out desperately seeking and desiring God's wisdom to protect me from the bad choices I was making. I was making wrong decisions that were hindering me from growing spiritually. How did I finally stop the mistakes and attain such wisdom? That takes a bit of explanation.

The Bible tells us that the Lord offers wisdom freely. Most people, however, do not bother to ask for it and therefore do not receive it. That was me. I simply did not know I could just ask for wisdom. Was it just that simple? Yes. Wisdom is a crop that is plentiful, but do we search for it, finding it where it thrives?

To embrace this divine gift, granted by God and readily available to any believer, we must ASK God for it through PRAYER. A profound verse that put me on a daily quest to ask God for His wisdom is James 1:5.

If anyone longs to be wise, ask God for wisdom and He will give it! He won't see your lack of wisdom as an opportunity to scold you over your failures, but He will overwhelm your failures with His generous grace. (James 1:5 TPT)

As clear as this verse is that our heavenly Father will not hold wisdom back from us, who will simply pray and ask God for such a thing? Not many. I never did. I just never knew it was that easy.

I began to pray for wisdom daily after I studied this verse. And my life changed when God gave me His wisdom to make the right choices along my daily path. When I realized His wisdom was something I needed, God showed me that acquiring this wisdom is like grace; it is something He offers, and we must receive it. It is something which He felt important enough to put in scripture, telling us to ask Him for it.

As a believer in Jesus who has accepted Him as your Lord and Savior and surrendered to Him through repentance, you can be assured that when you ask God for this gift of wisdom, He will give it to you and give it wholeheartedly.

Wisdom has everything to do with right and wrong and knowing what to do and when to do it. In my case, because I had made such terrible decisions resulting in severe consequences, I finally gave up my control. I surrendered my worldly wisdom and asked God for His wisdom, finally learning this better path to growth.

Cry out to God, as I did, and I assure you He will answer you. He will anoint you with His wisdom; the same wisdom talked about in His Word.

For The Lord gives wisdom; from His mouth come knowledge and understanding. (Proverbs 2:6 NIV)

The wisdom you will soon embrace is a gift that will enable you to fulfill God's will in your life. He will equip you to use this gift to glorify Him and for the good of others. Watch and see the wisdom that comes to you. It is a bountiful gift, a blessing available to all who ask for it. Just remember, ask the Lord God. It IS that simple.

> *How much better to get wisdom than gold, to get insight rather than silver!* (Proverbs 16:16 NIV)

. . . .

Kathleen M. Barrett

Kathleen Barrett is a published author and blogger, living on the Treasure Coast of Florida with Dennis, her husband of 52 years. She enjoys crafting stories that highlight how scripture is vital to healthy growth of spirit and soul, especially through life's many challenges. She has gleaned gems of wisdom from teaching all age levels, including women's groups. In the world of print media, she has enjoyed writing numerous articles in a variety of community news publications. Kathleen also wrote her own weekly neighborhood column while raising two children and volunteering as a summer recreation director. In addition, with three books to her credit, she gives thanks for all to the LORD.

On any given Sunday afternoon, you might just find this Italian girl preparing an Italian-Asian Fusion buffet feast for her multi-cultural family.

The following chapter, "Life's Course Corrections," describes one pivotal time in her young marriage when, what the enemy meant for evil, God meant for her good. She shares how you too, may Embrace the Journey on Your Path to Spiritual Growth.

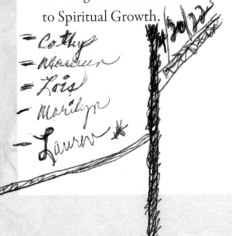

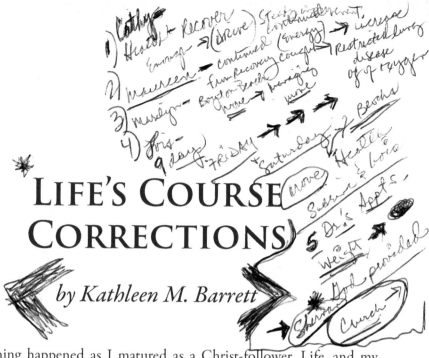

LIFE'S COURSE CORRECTIONS

by Kathleen M. Barrett

A funny thing happened as I matured as a Christ-follower. Life, and my sinful attitude, tapped me on the shoulder, reminding me that although I had accepted Jesus as my Savior, surrendering to Him as my LORD wasn't going to be as easy as following a flower-strewn path. Along the way, my life would need some course corrections!

You may think that your spiritual life is moving along nicely now that you've accepted Jesus as Savior. You go to church, fellowship with others, give your tithe and shout "Hallelujah!" at the appropriate times in service. You may even be a real prayer warrior. But then, you realize along the way that you are off-center from what your life in Christ ought to be. Something is not right. A course correction is needed.

On airplanes, there is an instrument called a course deviation indicator, which does just as its name implies. When the aircraft is flying to the left of the selected course, the needle deflects proportionally to the right. When the aircraft is flying right of the selected course, the needle deflects proportionally to the left. You can imagine that this type of indicator is necessary to help the pilot arrive safely at the planned destination.

Spiritually speaking, the Holy Spirit is a believer's "course deviation indicator." Growing as a Christian, I have come to depend on that still small voice "indicator", guiding and directing me as I trust His power for a perfect flight plan.

Today, as I write, God reminded me of how far he has brought me from a previous struggle I had with the spirits of offense and anger. In my Bible, a notation I had written years ago in the margin next to Matthew 8:26, about Jesus rebuking the winds and the waves and calming the sea, was to me a kiss from God. I had circled the word "calm," and penciled the following: "Calm: Just the way you have made me, Lord. Recently, I was angry, but I sinned not. I did not hold the offense and accepted H.B.'s apology."

Today, I am praising God for His patience with me. Always re-directing my path when needed for my good and His ultimate glory. I can assure you; He is guiding you too. Here is my story.

My journey toward freedom from the spirits of offense and anger began at the age of 23. I had encountered the LORD in my younger years, and He kept me from making grave mistakes of judgement. His protection was over me. But I never acknowledged the absolute need for Him in my life until the accident.

My bridal blush was still aglow when my fervor to be the best wife I could be was tested on Memorial Day weekend, 1969. Despite my asthmatic condition, the reason I stayed home from work that day, I tackled the ironing of my husband's twenty-three button-down collared shirts. I amazed myself as I finished each one, placing them on hangers, awaiting my husband's compliments.

Later in the afternoon, with asthma subsided, I made a run to the bank. Our kitten rode in the car with me, nervously pacing on the seat as I drove. I thought it strange when, on the way home from the bank, an eerie, unsettling feeling came over me. I brushed off the uneasiness. Years later, I would come to recognize that "uneasiness" as an alert signal from the Holy Spirit to pray.

I thought about what I would prepare for dinner for my hungry bridegroom, who would soon be arriving home from work. He was a carpenter, and I knew he would be tired after working all day on his current project - a high-rise condominium.

I received a phone call from my mom just as I entered the house, which changed my plans from a quiet dinner as newlyweds of just four months to a terrifying trip to the emergency room. My parents rushed me to my husband's side. Dennis lay barely conscious, waiting for an orthopedic surgeon to arrive.

Earlier in his workday, Dennis followed instructions to remove one of the ceiling forms from a room of a fifth-floor condo. Ceiling forms are the temporary wooden structures or supports that hold the ceiling in place after the cement has been poured. When he removed the one, all the other forms became loose and, like a domino effect, fell on him one after the other. The force and the movement of the collapse pushed him out of the unsecured exterior of the building.

To my horror, I learned that the man who had stood at the altar with me only four months earlier had fallen the entire five stories to the ground, feet first, onto a pile of cement blocks. He now lay on the gurney, feet swelling out of his work boots.

Four hours later, the surgeon arrived. Three days later, I went into shock. My parents rushed me to the emergency room at that same hospital. Dennis was on the fourth floor above me, with a broken back, both ankles crushed, and fighting for his life. Any memory of my own condition has since been forgotten. My mother, however, later told me that I was delirious before they got me to the hospital, laughing hysterically and blurting out all kinds of nonsensical sentences. My parents were a total support system to Dennis and me.

At the time of my life-altering event, what little faith I had was wrapped up in rosary beads and rituals. I would soon discover that God would show me just how much I needed Him as I pleaded to Him daily in the candle-lit chapel of Holy Cross Hospital.

> 1 John 5:14, *This is the confidence we have in approaching God: that if we ask anything according to his will, he hears us.* (NIV)

Dennis bore the confinement of a full body cast – torso, legs, and feet - during his painfully slow year of recuperation. Once Dennis shed the plaster, there were months of physical therapy necessary for him to learn how to walk with a newly fused ankle.

We spent our first year as newlyweds crafting. He built intricate plastic model ships, and when I wasn't at work, I did paint by numbers. That year God was crafting something of His own. In the eighth month of my husband's recovery, despite the restrictions of the casts, we discovered that we were pregnant with our first child. Who can understand God's ways?

> Isaiah 55:8-9, *"For my thoughts are not your thoughts. Nor are your ways My ways," declares the LORD. "For as the heavens are higher than the earth, so are My ways higher than your ways and My thoughts than your thoughts."* (NIV)

We were happily blessed with a healthy baby girl in October of 1970; and, two and a half years later, in May of 1973, with a healthy baby boy. The full weight of so many challenges and changes in less than five years was dizzying. Dennis had returned to work in a more stable field, utilities – allowing him to keep both feet on the ground! But my fragile emotions kept the family on a roller-coaster. No one knew what mood I would be in next. I realized at some point that I was tired of the conflict with the stranger within – always taking offense, angry and sad.

God always knows us best, and one thing He knew was that I needed a friend. I met a vivacious, carrot top of a Christian believer on a neighborhood home improvement board I had joined. This divine appointment I recognize as a significant course correction.

Over the many months we volunteered together, Tina invited me several times to attend church with her. Eventually, I could no longer make excuses. I was sinking lower daily - barely getting the kids off to school, then rushing home to hunker down with my drapes closed and boxes of tissues and chocolates nearby until it was time to pick them up from school. I was a hot and ugly mess. A course correction was vital.

I finally accepted Tina's invitation to go to church. The children and I attended her church from time to time, but I still wasn't sure about making a total commitment.

As for my husband, his involvement in church activity was not on the radar. He worked full time and on the weekends. He persevered, but I did not respect his efforts at the time. My anger seethed within because he was absent, both physically and emotionally. I longed for us to be yoked together in faith, attending church as a family.

In retrospect, I recognize the disunity between my husband and me was Satan's plan to sidetrack, frustrate, and destroy me. His plan almost worked. But why did I not realize that my "determined-to-provide-for-my-family" husband might be fighting demons of his own?

My emotional instability and selfishness blinded me to his struggles. I regret the friction, sadness, and unnecessary pain I caused myself and my family.

I continued to alternate weekends between my former church and this new spirit-filled congregation to which Tina had invited me. Gradually I felt drawn to the friendly fellowship and the teachings that came directly from the Bible.

I had found new life! My children did as well, becoming continually active in the youth group. There I eventually made the vital step of publicly declaring my faith by adult water Baptism in May of 1985. Baptism was the vital course correction appointed and anointed by God. My children received baptism as young adults. My beloved husband eventually went to the altar and accepted Jesus as Savior. As a family, we served at our home church for 27 years.

> Proverbs 3:5,6 (NIV), *Trust in the LORD with all your heart and lean not on your own understanding; in all your ways acknowledge him, and he will make your paths straight.*

I knew that verse in my head, but it had not quite settled in my heart. Even with my public confession of faith, I had a lot of "trusting and acknowledging" to do as I grew to make Jesus my Lord.

The enemy was relentless. The spirit of offense clung to me. I was easily angered when I perceived an insult or injury. I was right, and everyone else was wrong. I rejected and disrespected the opinions and advice of others, which I blamed on my heritage. After all, my beloved Italian mother always had the right answer. My hot, quick temper was also a "gift" of my Italian roots. God's truth revealed to me that both behaviors were products of my own emotional immaturity. Offense and anger do not reflect Christlike character, and I was made in the image of God. The Holy Spirit's nudge set me on another necessary course correction. Scripture says I don't need to be right but righteous, esteeming others more highly than myself.

> Philippians 2:3,5 (NIV), *Do nothing out of selfish ambition or vain conceit, but in humility consider others better than yourselves. Your attitude should be the same as that of Christ Jesus.*

Through that nudging, I came to understand the Apostle Paul's instruction to believers and his reference to "shining stars" in Philippians 2:12-15 (NIV). "Therefore, my dear friends, ...continue to work out your salvation with fear and trembling, for it is God who works in you to will and to act according to his good purposes. Do everything without complaining, or arguing, so that you may become blameless and pure children of God without fault in a crooked and depraved generation, in which you shine like stars in the universe as you hold out the word of life."

I want to be a "shining star" in God's eyes! I came to realize that God allows life-changing events as a means of repentance and growth where needed. And I sure needed to repent. I needed to repent from those years of harboring anger and bitterness for what could have been if the accident had not happened.

I needed to repent from the years of allowing the spirit of offense to whisper lies like, *okay, he is well enough now, and I have needs, I want this, and I want that, and I know I deserve what I ask for.* My pity party had no end! Even when nothing was going wrong in my life, I would conjure up something to complain about! I discovered that my personality, strangely and sinfully, thrived in crisis. Slamming doors and running off somewhere, anywhere to massage my pain, I thought was the answer, but it was not. Leaving my two young children standing at the front window watching me drive away, not to return for hours, haunts me still.

Through professional counseling and healing prayer sessions, I learned to let go of haughty anger and wrong attitudes.

As the Lord continued to be patient with me, Psalm 51:4 spoke loud and clear.

> *Against You, You only, have I sinned and done what is evil in your sight, so that you are proved right when you speak and justified when you judge.* (NIV)

You might say I was pulled up by the bootstraps of conviction.

I offend my Savior when I hold a grudge against someone who has offended me. I offend my Savior when I get easily angered and shut down emotionally for days on end or take flight as I used to do. How can I dare to offend my Savior when He bore the burden of my sin? Every time I repeat a sin that harms myself or another, I am crucifying Jesus again and again.

 In a lesson regarding the doctrine of repentance in a Bible Study Fellowship group I attend, the notes highlighted a great point, "God is being kind when He makes us face our sin so that we will seek our Savior." If being faced with our sin is not a life course correction, I do not know what is!

Our own sinfulness is never pleasant to face, but in the light of God's kindness, can we do anything less than repent when the Holy Spirit convicts us of sin? Faced with the following verse, I had no choice but to repent, understanding that I am a sinner saved by grace and continuing in sin is repugnant to God. "Or do you show contempt for the riches of his kindness, tolerance, and patience, not realizing that God's kindness leads you toward repentance?" Romans 2:4 (NIV)

You see, I came to understand that it is not enough to confess Jesus as Savior and be baptized. I had to prove my love and commitment by aligning my will with His. A course correction of my heart was needed, taking on His characteristics and obeying the principles in His Word. Galatians 5:22 became my checklist of progress.

> But the fruit of the Spirit is love, joy, peace, patience, kindness, goodness, faithfulness, gentleness and self-control. (NIV)

How do you go from sincerely declaring Jesus as Savior to committing to Him as LORD? Remembering His unmerited kindness and patience towards us unyielding and immature humans is a good place to start. Also, having an open, willing, and teachable spirit will allow the Holy Spirit to have leeway to direct your personal course correction. Are you willing to be led by the Spirit, do you have a teachable spirit or do you resist the Lord's correction?

I determined that if I were going to be a true, confessing Christ-follower, His excellent character would be the model for my life, and I would not put Him to shame.

The legacy I want to leave for my family must reflect Christ Jesus' character changes in me. Through the adversity in our lives, my faith has made me whole and healed because of Christ alone. A faith I pray will inspire my children and their children's children to grow in wisdom and grace and in favor with God and man. I must leave them a heritage of faith!

I no longer meditate on what "could have been" in my life. Instead, I meditate on the Word of God and on the joy that He has restored in my life. This natural life will never be perfect. But God's perfect love toward me restored the lost years.

Spiritual growth is a life-long process. Watch for God's course corrections in your life. As God takes you from glory to glory, do not resist the method He uses! He wants to be more than Savior to you. He wants to be your LORD. He has your best interest at heart. You are the bride of His desire. The one for whom He promises to return. Allow Him to do the deep and necessary work in you before you meet your Bridegroom face to face.

If you are unsure about what needs refinement in your character, ask the Holy Spirit, according to Psalm 139:24, "See if there is any offensive way in me and lead me in the way everlasting." (NIV)

I am thankful that God cares enough about my character to even reveal past unconfessed sin to me. He is not finished with me yet, and He is not finished with you either. He is reaching down, waiting for you to reach up. Repent, and enjoy the freedom from wrong attitudes and guilt you will soon experience as you become a committed Christ-follower. Embrace God's course corrections for your life! Allow Him to blossom you in the sometimes tangly mess of life's challenges and trials. His Lordship will take you safely to your destination.

EMBRACE COMPASSION

by Kimberly Ann Hobbs

According to the Bible, we know that God is a compassionate God, slow to anger, abounding in love and faithfulness. (Psalm 86:15) Like all of God's attributes, His compassion is infinite and eternal. His compassions never fail; they are new every morning. (Lamentations 3:22-23)

What does this word compassion mean for us, and how can we understand the importance of embracing such a word? I will use a biblical example.

When Jesus was asked what the greatest commandment was, He responded that the greatest commandment is to love God with all our heart, mind, and strength. But He added the second commandment, which is very important: 'love your neighbor as yourself.' (Matthew 22:34-40)

The Bible is clear that compassion is an attribute of God and of God's people as well. We would do well, therefore, to heed the commands of our Lord and embrace this word on our path to spiritual growth.

We can all learn to be compassionate right where we are. You are a witness for Christ by your life, attitude, and love and compassion toward people – regardless of their race, religion, or ethnic background. If we put our hands and feet to the gospel message and live it out each day, those around us will see our love and understand we are compassionate to one another.

Be kind and compassionate to one another, forgiving each another, just as in Christ God forgave you. (Ephesians 4:32 NIV)

As we walk through our lives, we encounter humans who are rough, ugly, beaten down, and in need of love. How can we ignore anyone in need by "turning a blind eye" when God clearly instructs us to be compassionate? We cannot. We need to work on this in our close connections as well as when we encounter someone with needs along life's path. The need may not always come as the widow or orphan that needs your compassionate heart to give money or go to a foreign country to serve, although their needs are to be attended to as God's Word instructs. You may have to work at being aware of those in closer proximity, intentionally being aware of the needs directly in your path.

You may live with a very needy person who continually asks for help all throughout your day. Or you may have an extended family member you do not desire to visit or call because they are a constant complainer. It is not easy to rise to compassion for someone who talks only of their problems and continues with the same story that does not change. You may have a crippled neighbor who struggles to get out, but you are too busy to help, so you look the other way. As a chosen child of God, we must kindly smile, gather our strength, lend an understanding ear, forgive them for their complaints and reach out to help them, extending our time and embracing compassion with a loving heart.

You are always and dearly loved by God! So, robe yourself with virtues of God, since you have been divinely chosen to be holy. Be merciful as you endeavor to understand others, and be compassionate, showing kindness toward all. Be gentle and humble, unoffendable in your patience with others. Tolerate the weaknesses of those in the family of faith, forgiving them in the same way you have been graciously forgiven by Jesus Christ. If you find fault with someone, release this same gift of forgiveness to them. (Colossians 3:12-13 TPT)

We must strive for true spiritual maturity as we follow this journey of life. Some things may not be easy for us to accomplish, but as we grow spiritually on this journey to excellence, seeking after God's heart, we will see more and more how gracious and merciful our Lord is. God's love is shown to us in infinite ways as we follow His example through our day-to-day life. He will provide you with strength, time, love, and wisdom to do all that you are called to do.

— PRAYER REQUESTS — 4/27/22

✗ CHRISTY → (MT ↗ TONA)

LOIS — MOVING / GOD'S STRENGTH   4-DAY WEDDING
        CAR ISSUES →   GORDON MARRIED
        JOB RESPONSIBILITIES   7← LAUDERDALE
    — FRIDAY — 3PM
    — SATURDAY — SATURDAY EVENING →
            12 NOON
            10:30 AM

SABRINA → HEALTH ISSUES → GOD NEEDS TO INTERVENE

MAUREEN → SAFE TRIP —
    CONTINUED HEALING / PRAISES

Cheryl — PRAISES → ($200 / MCR) →
        QUIET WEEK / ALLERGIES /

Christy → JAVIER; LUWETT
        104 YEAR OLD — GRANDFATHER
        KEEP IN PRAYERS /   ASKING   SEEKING
        COSTA RICA; TUESDAY → QUESTIONS   THE
                               CLOSER   LORD

MARILYN → MOVE SMOOTHLY → ALL IS WELL.

LAUREN — BUSY SEASON →

CATHY → HEALTH; WORK   DEIRDRA — NEXT SATURDAY

Diesha
Cathy
Carolyn

Vaishali Nair

is an assertive pharmaceutical expert. For 24 years, she has worked in manufacturing, research & development, technology transfer, and project management in the pharmaceutical business based out of Mumbai, India. Vaishali has led project deliveries of 60+ complex, innovative, breakthrough projects working with cross-functional APAC, EU, US teams across the globe in pharma giants like Sandoz (Novartis), Janssen India, and Pfizer, winning numerous recognitions and awards.

She is blessed with an equally dynamic husband and two grown children, with whom she loves spending quality time. She also enjoys singing, encouraging and motivating others, and contributing and volunteering for numerous Indian non-profit organizations for underprivileged children and physically challenged and disabled people.

Vaishali's spiritual journey with Jesus through the diverse Indian culture inspires many who fear proclaiming Jesus as their saviour. She can have all the excuses in the world not to serve God, but Vaishali passionately puts her relationship with Christ first and serves Him wholeheartedly.

To know more about Vaishali and her spiritual growth, please visit her Facebook page @EnduringGenesis and follow her on Instagram @vaishali.nair.18

Driven

LEADERSHIP
* of American group
- Women in the window)
- WW Leaders

JESUS IS THE WAY ...
YES, THE ONLY WAY!

by Vaishali Nair

We never know our destiny on our own, but God knows what His will is and what plan He has for us. Our eternal Father works out HIS purpose for our life on this earth even before He plants us in the womb of our biological mothers. He revealed this to me in 50 years of my life, and my heart knows that He will continue fulfilling His plan with love and care until I have eternal life with him.

I was born and brought up in Mumbai, a metropolitan city of India. My parents were a happily married, working couple. They were very kind and spiritually-inclined people who cared for many people and fulfilled their responsibilities selflessly for their parents, children, extended families, and family friends - without any expectations in return. I was the youngest of four siblings. When I was nine years old, God put few questions into my heart that I had never asked anyone in my family. I was curious to know why my mom had such a close relationship with Jesus. I had seen her praying to Jesus, reading the Holy Bible often, and visiting church on some Sunday mornings, even though she was not a born-again Christian. I recollect one Sunday morning when I asked her about my elder brother. I was so eager to know why he was not able to talk and walk like normal kids. She opened her heart that day and told me how the enemy took out his weapon on a God-loving family. My brother was hit by a polio attack when he was three years old. My parents tried all the best treatments from the best doctors, just wanting to hear his voice and see him playing like other kids. They even visited temples of various gods in India and worshipped them for his healing. The enemy had blinded them so they would not get closer to Jesus, the true Lord.

One of Mom's closest Christian friends had insisted that my mother visit a nearby church and pray to Jesus to heal her dumbstruck child. In those years, a non-Christian woman visiting a church was not easily accepted by the Indian community. But God spoke to her that night, and she took her first courageous step of faith to visit the church. She cried out loud in pain and prayed to Jesus, asking Him to heal her son. The next day, when she was about to lift my brother in her arms, my brother called her "Mom" in a soft voice - after four years of his speechless existence. He then moved in her arms on his own! Our Father had healed him miraculously. God, our Lord, is so great and kind!! She accepted Jesus as her Saviour on the same day. Her faith increased in Jesus day by day as He answered many of her prayers in her stillness.

This was the first time Jesus God opened his arms for me, too. I realized Mom was right and that Jesus is loving, kind, and He heals us in His glory. That was the beginning of my journey.

> *Nevertheless, I will bring health and healing to it; I will heal my people and will let them enjoy abundant peace and security.* (Jeremiah 33:6 NIV)

As God starts lifting you on His path, the enemy really wants you to believe that Jesus is not your Saviour. He tries to paralyse your faith, make you too weak to follow Jesus, and tempts you to leave Jesus and be his slave for life. He tried to do the same to me too.

My mother continued building her relationship with God through faith, worship, and prayer. My dad did not accept God initially because he had different religious beliefs. When I was 12 years old, I remember my dad arguing with my mom, asking her not to read the Holy Bible. He told her not to speak about Jesus in our home. This made her sad, and she tried to explain to him the good work of the Lord in their lives. My dad, in the heat of the argument, tore apart her Bible and threw it in the backyard. That rainy, windy night was so difficult for me. The enemy was at his best, trying to challenge the existence of God in my mind. He planted a very toxic thought in my heart and made me wonder whether Jesus was really a true God. If He was, then why did He make my parents argue over His existence, and why couldn't my mom convince my dad about God's unconditional love, and why was my dad reluctant to accept God's place in his life?

I was so young that I did not know that the enemy was trying to pull me apart from my loving God. The next day was bright, but my heart wasn't - it was broken by grief and sadness and filled with toxic thoughts. In that moment, the Holy Spirit gave me the wisdom to act. I searched for those beautiful golden pages of the Bible, deciding that I would stick them back together. I knew that my mom would be very happy to receive her Bible back when she returned from work.

After searching for an hour, I could not find a single page. I blamed the windy night and sat there with my doubts about God. I cried to God to reveal Himself to me, but there was no response. As I got up to go back inside, I saw a very tiny piece of paper from the Bible. It had only a few words printed in the smallest font. Those words had a profound impact on my heart and changed my entire life. My mom had told me that whenever you open any random page of Bible, it will speak to you, answer you, teach you, and guide you. I witnessed that at that very moment. The tiny paper read "'They are joined fast to one another; they cling together and cannot be parted." Job 41:17 (NIV). I jumped with joy because that was the truth I needed to hear. Not only did this refer to the pages of the Bible, but to the fact that Jesus had joined Himself, through faith, to me and my parents. The words of God remain forever. That was the first time Jesus spoke to me so directly through His words, and I accepted Him as my Saviour, my Lord, and my loving Father that very moment.

I shared my experience with my mom that night. She thanked God for getting her precious daughter closer to Him.

My Saviour never left me thereafter. He has become a true companion and the Holy Spirit has guided me at every stage, through the challenges of life, leading me to live a spiritual life.

God is great, and so are His ways! He sees to it that His chosen ones are always on the correct path. Proverbs 4:3-4 NIV tells us,

> For I too was a son to my father,
>   still tender, and cherished by my mother.
> Then he taught me, and he said to me,
>   "Take hold of my words with all your heart;
> keep my commands, and you will live."

Years passed... My mother's teaching from the Bible, discussions about Jesus, prayer with her friends in our home, testimonies, and desire to serve the poor and needy greatly impacted me. My faith in Jesus intensified day by day. I was a shy, peace-loving girl, brilliant in my academics and sports. My parents always wanted me to be a doctor, but God compelled me to pursue my undergraduate degree in pharmacy. I was fascinated by the science of medicine that relieves pain, heals the sick, and saves lives. God nudged me to work in the area of research to develop pioneering medicine to serve humankind. I understood years later why I never imagined myself as a doctor. When I read about Jesus' crucifixion, tears roll down my face. My heart feels the pain of His wounds, and I cry as I think about how He shed his blood to wash our sins. God knew I would not be able to see blood, so He gave me wisdom to choose pharmacy over medical. It was His plan to protect me like a loving Father and yet use me to fulfill His purpose for my life.

For it is God who works in you to will and to act to fulfill his good purpose. (Philippians 2:13 NIV)

God chalked out a new journey when I fell in love at the age of 18 and married the love of my life at 24. Having Ravi as my husband added a new dimension as I adopted a new Hindu culture after marriage and learnt to share my life with my in-laws. It required getting used to understanding a completely different language (Malayalam) from the southern part of India, a distinct Hindu religion, diverse culture and rituals, and radical shifts in my diet. Everything was so different and new, but I embraced the journey. God was with me, encouraging my every step of building new extended relationships successfully through this marriage. It was not easy, but God allowed me to walk through these experiences because He had a bigger picture of my life. I accepted everyone and everything wholeheartedly and got accustomed to all Hindu rituals. However, I continued praying to my Lord Jesus for all His blessings on me and my family. On the outside, I was standing with folded hands in front of idols, but in my inner soul, I was praying to Jesus. There were a few occasions when I was challenged by my own emotions and feelings for my faith in Jesus. Sometimes there was an internal tug of war between my beliefs and those of my sweetheart. I would seek Jesus for guidance, never wanting to hurt the feelings of my loving and caring husband because his happiness was more important to me. Every time God showed me that the rituals were part of my journey, but He wanted me to focus on loving those in my life as Jesus would.

And now these three remain: faith, hope and love. But the greatest of these is love. (1 Corinthians 13:13 NIV)

In 1997, God filled our broken hearts left from a miscarriage when He blessed us with our sweet little daughter, Anuprita. She was indeed a miracle baby of Lord Jesus as I had experienced many issues during the pregnancy.

All was going well, and I was happily juggling work and family life. Then, in 2000, my happy world came crashing down when I lost my precious loving mom. I was just 29 years old, and she left a void that I thought nobody would fill. God knew me so well, and He wrapped us in His loving arms as He blessed us with a baby boy, Anuraag. As he has grown, his thoughtfulness and caring ways often remind me of my mom.

Losing my mom is one of the deepest sorrows my heart will carry. I know she is happy sitting at the feet of our heavenly Father. Her goodness, caring, and tremendous love for Jesus till the end of her life will live on – a spiritual legacy from generation to generation. Her life made me realize the huge responsibility of being a mother - giving moral values and passing on spiritual values of faith to my children. Everything happens for a reason. That is what God taught me in the reproductive season of my life.

Start children off on the way they should go, and even when they are old, they will not turn from it. (Proverbs 22:6 NIV)

My Lord has always been with me and continued to pursue me. In the midst of a busy life when my responsibility at work was increasing, there was a period of time when the enemy attacked me relentlessly, attempting to take my vibrant, God-gifted energy. He used all his tools and strategies to bring down my morale, including making my relationships bitter, creating roadblocks in my career, and creating misunderstandings between my husband and me. At times I was shaken but remained under His wings, praying to Jesus and the Holy Spirit to guide me. The Holy Spirit filled me with power and strength, refilling the empty, drained vessels inside me. I completely surrendered to Exodus 14:14 (NIV), "The Lord will fight for you; you need only to be still."

The enemy did not spare opportunities and created situations to tempt me to retaliate and make things worse, but God gave me the strength to keep myself calm and remain patient as I waited for the devil to give up.

After this worst season in my life, God wanted to heal me completely and claim me as His own. He knew my heart desired to heal in His presence, away from everything I had been going through. Jesus gave me that opportunity. I got a very good leadership assignment with a pharma multinational giant Pfizer in the city of Vizag, which was quite far away from Mumbai. I needed to relocate away from my family, to live among strangers who spoke a language I did not know. I moved to Vizag on 16th June 2018. During this time, Jesus miraculously planted people in my life who believed in Him, like my driver. I was not aware that he was Jesus' faithful servant during my days in Vizag; I only came to know about it on the day of my departure.

One day, when I was exploring the city, my car suddenly stopped on the road. I gazed out of the window, waiting for my driver to check what was wrong, and I saw a signboard that said "Jesus Calls." It was advertising a Christian ministry that I had donated some money to for few years, but I had never interacted with anyone in the ministry. I decided to visit the office. I was welcomed by a kind and humble woman with whom I could not interact much as I did not know the local language. I sat there and prayed to Jesus in the chapel, feeling peaceful. When I was about to leave, an older woman came near me, and she hugged me. Her touch was the same as my mom's, and I got goosebumps when I saw her face. She looked exactly like my mom. Later, she told me that her only daughter, who was in the USA, looked like me. When she showed me her photo, I was amazed at God's work. She did resemble me. What a miracle of Jesus! I got my mom, and she got her daughter. His ways are miraculous. I spent most of my evenings with this my new mom. We shopped together, dined together, and spent good quality time talking about Jesus and His ministry.

God healed me with love and care within that short span of one and a half months.

I know now that He is the one and only one who loves me from the heart, and I am His precious child. My loving Father has helped me realise who He is. He directed me to my goals and His vision and corrected my self-limiting beliefs. He made me completely new in His faith. This was a phenomenal transformation and the wisest decision of my life. God nurtured me through His blessings and teachings, never allowing me to slip from my moral values, which were gifts from Him. I understood the precious gifts of the Holy Spirit, which I already had but had never understood. He directed me to my hobbies of singing and writing, inducing joy and happiness in my life. He put my closest cousin sister as a prayer warrior in my path who helped me understand Him better through prayer, worship, and our conversations. God showered me as His most loving child.

And it will be said: "Build up, build up, prepare the road! Remove the obstacles out of the way of my people." (Isaiah 57:14 NIV)

I was in awe of His glory and decided to offer myself to Him, to serve Him through the remaining years of my life. I knew I must do this but did not how.

One day, I came across a Facebook live session with Kimberly Hobbs from Women World Leaders. She was asking women around the globe to share beautiful stories of their lives leading to victories in Jesus' name. In that perfect moment, I realized the purpose of my life. It was to serve women around the globe. I joined the WWL Facebook group the same day. I came into contact with so many beautiful women in this group who have thoughts, dreams, and goals to serve Jesus. That made my soul much stronger and more courageous. God brought me onto the leadership team of this ministry within two months, and He gave me the opportunity to share my spiritual journey and how I grew in Jesus.

In the process, the enemy again struck me as my husband tested positive for COVID in April 2021, but God saved him graciously without even a single complication. I felt God's presence, knowing He was watching over me and my children. The enemy did not give up, but he pushed me back with his second evil trap attack. I lost my father-in-law the day my husband became COVID negative, on the 20th day of April 2021. He tried to bring my strength down and make me feel low. He thought these distractions would deflect my faith and cause me to give up on my new mission to serve women across the globe. But I heard the groaning of the Holy Spirit so loudly inside me and even directly heard God's voice say, "In the stillness of darkness, who I am? I am your bright star." The words gave me tremendous hope beyond imagination, making my path clear and giving me the confidence to complete

His purpose in my life. My mother had taught me that when you try to get closer to God, the enemy attempts to trap you, so you should pray deeply and fervently to Jesus.

God is a strong protector who does not allow the enemy to touch your soul.

God provides for you beyond measure. He chose me to write and share this journey to encourage women around the globe to rely on His love, care, support, and strength to defeat the enemy, and to believe in His words and His existence.

> *In him we were also chosen, having been predestined according to the plan of him who works out everything in conformity with the purpose of his will.* (Ephesians 1:11 NIV)

The purpose of spiritual development is summed up well in Romans 12:2 (NIV) that exhorts us with these powerful words: "Do not conform to the pattern of this world but be transformed by the renewing of your mind. Then you will be able to test and approve what God's will is—his good, pleasing and perfect will." God's truth and purpose transform the soul, spirit, mind, and strength in all our activities. Everything we have, including our knowledge, skills, talents, and abilities, is to be stewarded to God. Spiritual development is increasingly aligning God's purposes for the world with our story.

As I embrace a new journey with Jesus, I know it will be full of challenges. But I also know for sure that His glory is more than enough to broaden my spiritual horizon as I follow His path. I am convinced of this because deep in my heart, **I know Jesus is the way and the only way to Eternal life!**

When I sit down to pray in early hours of morning,
I want to tell you something, O Lord!

When I sip from my coffee mug and plan for the day full of your affirmations,
I want to tell you something, O Lord!

When I look at my lovely children and the way they pray to you
Asking for blessings in all their lives
I want to tell you something, O Lord!

When I glance at my sweetheart , and he overlooks from his loving gaze
When he knows my love and worries without choosing the words
I want to tell you something, O Lord!

When I check on my friends and their wellbeing
When I encourage them to overcome life struggles
I want to tell you something, O Lord!

When I see the world around me
Waiting to see your glory everyday
I want to tell you something, O Lord!

When I know life is short and there is so much to do
When I know time will fly and it's time to fly towards you
I want to tell you something, O Lord!

When I know that you already knew what I had to tell you
When I know that you knew me before I existed
Still, I want to tell you something, O Lord!

I may not be there here for a long time
But keep my loved ones under your wings, O Lord!
Let them know you are the way and the only way, O Lord!
That's the only thing which I want to tell you, O Lord!

Embrace Righteousness

by Julie T. Jenkins

We've all heard the phrase, "Don't act so self-righteous," and yet society often screams at us to do what feels right, and the Bible commands us to live righteously. If you are confused, you are certainly justified!

Righteousness is doing what is right. The question is, who decides what is right? If we are most concerned about comfort, we will do what is right in our own eyes. If we are most concerned about popularity, we will do what is most acceptable to society. But as Christians, God wants us to do what is right in His eyes. And that is the kind of righteousness that the Bible teaches.

> *The Lord loves righteousness and justice; the earth is full of his unfailing love.* (Psalm 33:5 NIV)

It may seem futile to try to be righteous in God's eyes. I think that is why so many people give up and do what feels good or what will earn them the praise of society. Only God Himself is perfectly righteous, and so it can seem impossible to please Him. After all, we are born sinful, the Bible chronicles that the first man and woman sinned, and I know I sinned before eating breakfast today! The Old Testament tells of the Pharisees who added man-made law upon man-made law to God's law, seeking to never step outside the scope of righteousness, and even they failed. Romans 3:10 declares *There is no one righteous, not even one. (NIV)*

So, where does that leave us? How are we supposed to embrace the righteousness of God?

The key is that we must realize we will never be righteous using our own will and power, but instead, God offers us the opportunity to clothe ourselves in the righteousness of Jesus Christ.

Jesus came to earth and lived a sinless life. He was perfectly righteous. And then He died a sinner's death, taking on the sins of all of humanity and paying the price of death. You and I have the opportunity to accept His payment on our behalf, claiming His righteousness as a free gift. The apostle Paul teaches us, *Christ's love compels us, because we are convinced that one died for all... that those who live should no longer live for themselves but for him who died for them and was raised again. ... Therefore if anyone is in Christ, the new creation has come: The old has gone, the new is here! ... God made him who had no sin to be sin for us, so that in him we might become the righteousness of God.* (2 Cor 5:14-15, 17, 21 NIV)

We can embrace the righteousness of God by embracing Christ Himself! To do so, pray this prayer:

Dear Most Holy and Loving God, I confess that I have sinned, and I ask for your forgiveness. I am a sinner who has rightly been separated from you. But God, today I turn to you, thanking you for the gift of your Son, Jesus, who died a sinner's death that I might live forever in communion with you. Your flesh was mutilated that I might receive your covering of righteousness. Jesus, I thank you for your sacrifice for me. I humbly accept the gift of your life that you so lovingly gave for me and claim my place in your kingdom for eternity. Help me hold my head high as one who follows your way, not the way of the devil or the world or as one who attempts to live in my own self-righteousness. From this moment on, I live my life for you! In Jesus' name, I pray, Amen.

If you have just prayed that prayer – Congratulations! All of heaven is rejoicing! But just a word of warning, this doesn't mean your life will be easy. However, it does mean that you can repeatedly turn to God when you come up against sin or strife. Call on Him. He will empower you, forgive you, and best of all, walk beside you as He grows you in personal righteousness even as you display the righteousness of God through the blessing of Jesus Himself!

But thanks be to God that, though you used to be slaves to sin, you have come to obey from your heart the pattern of teaching that has now claimed your allegiance. You have been set free from sin and have become slaves to righteousness. (Romans 6:17-18 NIV)

Sara Sahm

was born in Orange County, California but grew up a country girl riding horses, playing in the mud, and going to church. As a child, her favorite quote was, "I love Jesus, and the devil is an idiotic brat." From a very young age, she dreamed of sharing God's Word through music and word. Through many ups and downs, that dream has become a reality. "To write for WWL and have an online ministry is a dream come true," she says. Sara enjoys writing, not for the million readers, but for the one-in-a-million who needs to hear what she wrote. She credits God's never-ending relentless love for all she has today. Sara resides in Jupiter, Florida, with her husband Doug, two daughters, two dogs, a cat, and a bearded dragon named Watermelon. When she isn't escaping into the tranquility of her music studio, she can be found scrapbooking, paddle boarding, and playing with her family. Sara's music can be found on her website, sarasahmmusic.com

HE WHISPERS WORTHY

by Sara Sahm

> For we are a MASTERPIECE.
> He has created us anew in Christ Jesus,
> So we can do the good things He planned for us long ago.
> (Ephesians 2:10 NLV)

It was 1987. I remember that day so well, sitting on the grassy knoll at my little school. Right then, I knew I was a child of God; He whispered, "worthy, chosen, loved." He gave me a purpose to serve and sing, and I believed, with all my heart, that I was worthy of such a privilege.

> "For I know the plans I have for you," declares the Lord, "plans to prosper you and not to harm you, plans to give you hope and a future." (Jeremiah 29:11 NIV)

Even though I didn't know that much about Jesus, I knew I was loved. And I knew He was with me always. The first Bible verse I ever learned was Psalm

23. "Even though I walk through the valley of the shadow of death, I will fear no evil, for you are with me." (Psalm 23:4 ESV) God knew how much I would need to remember that truth.

At the age of 13, I developed bulimia. By the time I was 18, I was so hopeless and controlled by the disease that I tried to kill myself. I questioned my worth and my identity, and I questioned God's love for me. I felt dirty and worthless and ashamed. I hated my reflection in the mirror, and I hated my body, but really looking back, I just hated the lies I'd begun to believe about myself. Lies like: "You're unlovable," and "You're pathetic and will never amount to anything." I had forgotten what God said about me. I had replaced "fearfully and wonderfully made" (Psalm 139:14 NIV) with "afraid and worthless."

It wasn't long after graduating high school that my life really began to fall apart. I was running from God as fast as I could. I felt lost and without purpose. I tried to convince myself that everything I had believed about God was a lie. I remember screaming at God to leave me alone. I just wanted to not feel, but my soul was longing for the Lord, and in that longing, I felt so much pain. 1 Corinthians 6:19 speaks about how once we have the Holy Spirit dwelling in us, we are no longer our own but a temple of the Lord. I was the Lord's temple, and at the same time, I was trying to deny the temple existed. This constant conflict left me feeling crazy, hopeless, and confused.

By the time I was 23, I was the deepest I'd ever been in my eating disorder. I was purging ten or more times a day. I couldn't keep an apple down, and I knew every clean single-stall bathroom in town. I wanted to leave my boyfriend, but each time I tried, he would lock me in, and it would turn into a raging fight. I was so sick, and I wanted out. But with the high price of rehab and therapy, I saw no possible solution. My self-worth had hit such a low that when my boyfriend asked me to enter the adult entertainment world with him, it seemed like a good idea. I seriously considered it. But in my spirit,

I knew I couldn't actually live that life. Yes, I had wandered so far from my purpose, but that was a distance I wasn't willing to travel. My boyfriend was angry, and after that, things began to deteriorate rapidly. I was angry that he would even consider having me do pornography, and yet I felt honored at the same time. I had such a disoriented sense of love and self-worth that it was hard to know what to feel. But I knew I needed to leave. The umbilical cord of worth had been severed. But hope for my life was not gone because God was still writing my story.

I was working for a construction company at the time, and one morning I was at work all alone. I cried out to God, saying, "God help! I can't do this! What do I do?" I turned on the computer and searched, "affordable eating disorder treatment." A place popped up. It was located in San Diego - near my mom, and it was not expensive. I felt hope for the first time in a long time. I marveled, "Wow, what a great coincidence!" Today, I recognize that moment as an answered prayer. God had met me where I was and gave me something to hope for. "God's gift"

After a long month of waiting, I arrived at the treatment facility. I was terrified! My eating disorder had become my identity. When I was sad, nervous, or lonely, it was where I ran. Everyone who knew me wanted to help me and save me. I had become accustomed to the victim role, and while I wanted freedom from bulimia, I was also afraid of what that would look like. Who would I be then? Would God forgive me? What would I do with my life? I'd forgotten how to live, how to love, and how to be loved.

Have you ever lost self worth tied to something?

The first phone call I was able to make was to a woman I had met at church. She had always been like a big sister. She encouraged me in the Lord and always reminded me of what He said about me. We hadn't spoken in about five years, but it was like that time wasn't lost when she picked up the phone. Right away, she reminded me of God's love for me. She encouraged me to seek Him, pray, and let Him back into the places in my heart that I had sealed off tight.

job
life
behavior
family
children
husband

possessions

I leaned on my Bible. I cried, I journaled, and I fought! Daily, I got on my knees and cried to God. I would hide away in the closet when we had alone time and just read and write what God was telling me. In those moments, He reminded me of His promises. He reminded me who I was in Him: loved, beautiful, special, and wanted. The Lord reawakened the calling to serve that He had placed in my heart on that grassy knoll when I was just a little girl.

The turning point came the day God showed me that my eating disorder was all based on lies. In my journal, I wrote, "Fear is a lie that holds us imprisoned, apart from the life we were meant to live." At that moment, I realized that if fear is a lie, then the truth is love. And if God is love, then I needed to start learning His truth so I could replace the lies and no longer be afraid. This truth that the Holy Spirit spoke to me was mind-blowing for me.

God showed me through His Word that I had been looking for worth in all the wrong places. I had put my hope in looks, people, and accomplishments, but I had not placed my worth in Him. My eating disorder had begun out of a desire to feel a sense of worth, but instead, it had become a deadly obsession that ended up controlling me and drawing me away from the calling that God had given me. I had been looking for worth outside of God's will, outside of God's truth, which only led me to feelings of worthlessness. Matthew 6:33 (ESV) says, "But seek first the kingdom of God and his righteousness, and all these things will be added to you." Finally, I had found the truth that would lead me back to joy, health, and life.

> *The thief comes only to steal and kill and destroy; I have come that they may have life, and have it to the full.* (John 10:10 NIV)

I'm grateful for the trials I have survived. Without them, I wouldn't be the person I am today. Even Paul came to understand through his trials that the thorn in his flesh was something to rejoice in. He asked God to remove it, but

God reminded him that his struggles were allowed by God so that he would be dependent upon His grace alone. (2 Corinthians 12:7-10)

Learning how to see God's grace in every situation is not always easy. But doing so allows us to live in humility and accept that our worth can only be found in Him. Our weakness, our trials, and our pain give us the opportunity to point others towards the goodness of God's sufficient grace. When we depend on the Lord for our strength, we glorify Him. Every tear is an opportunity for victory. In every weakness, His strength shines! Finding worth becomes less about us and more about our Savior. "In all things God may be glorified through Jesus Christ." (1 Peter 4:11. ASV)

When I first began to contemplate what it is to find my identity in Christ, I thought It was more about what I did, including going to church, reading my Bible, and serving. But as I grew spiritually, I realized that my identity in Christ is not about what I do but is solely based on what Jesus has already done. I wanted to earn God's love, but I never could be good enough to earn it. Ephesians 2:8-9 ESV says, "For by grace you have been saved, through faith. And this is not your own doing; it is a gift from God, not a result of works, so that anyone may boast." His sacrifice, grace, and truth is enough. Unless our joy and worth are found in what He did and not on what we do, we will always feel empty. Trying to measure up to the world's standards of worth will only lead us to lives of emptiness.

The world tells us that we will find worth when: when we have the perfect home, the perfect marriage, the perfect body, car, or purse. We are told that these things will give us worth, define our identity, and bring us joy. I grew up shopping at thrift stores, and I've worn designer gowns. I have lived in a shack and a mansion. I have driven an $800 car that squeaked around every corner and owned a Mercedes. I thought I'd feel like I was worth something once I had the house, the car, and the clothes. But when I did, I still felt the same. I was still the little girl who felt worthless and still didn't feel like I belonged.

I only found worth when I began to seek my identity in Christ. Not until I humbled myself before the Lord and said, "I am unworthy and unable," did I find worth and strength.

We all have worth and purpose every day we wake up and choose to live our life with Jesus Christ as Lord and Savior of our lives. 2 Timothy 1:9 NIV says, "He has saved us and called us to a holy life—not because of anything we have done but because of his own purpose and grace. This grace was given us in Christ Jesus before the beginning of time." If you have given your life to Christ, you are part of that "US" that Paul is writing to Timothy about – you are a believer who has been called. And if you've not given your life to Christ, you can be assured that God is calling you right now. To be called implies wanted, and if something is wanted, it has worth. We know that we are wanted and have worth, not because of anything we have done, but because we have been given a gift of grace for God's purpose. We have been loved and wanted since before the beginning of time. That's a really powerful thought - take that in and receive it!

You are called, wanted, and have a God-given purpose. You are loved and have received all these things because of God's neverending and boundless grace. So close your eyes and listen for the whispers of your worth as you explore God's Word, pray, and grow. Sometimes whispers are loud, and sometimes they are quiet. But a whisper is still a whisper and when God whispers, His voice roars throughout creation. We are all called to glorify God with our lives. Striving to live in a manner worthy of our Lord is where true worth is found.

I encourage you to allow God into the deepest part of your heart. He will whisper worth. Be in the Word, be in prayer, and spend time listening until you are so close to His voice that His whisper becomes an undeniable roar of truth. If you know your calling, let God lead you in it. When things get tough, remind Him of His promises. If you are still waiting for the dream in your heart, expect it to happen in His perfect timing. If you don't know your calling, know that you have a purpose in His kingdom that will be revealed at the perfect moment. You may already be living it every day and not recognizing the importance of what you already do. Pray, wait, and know that there is no part too small and no part is more important than another. The Kingdom of God has many parts, and no part can stand alone. All are essential, and all have worth.

> *As a prisoner for the Lord, then, I urge you to live a life worthy of the calling you have received.* (Ephesians 4:1 NIV)

We can remain a prisoner chained to our past and our fear, or we can choose to be a prisoner of the Lord. We have choice! He has made the way for us already. So assume your position and start living a life worthy of the calling you have received. You are worth it!

Today, by the grace of God, I have an incredible husband and two precious little girls. I can say I love myself and have been set free from my eating disorder. I know who God says I am. I still get attacked, but I'm learning how to fight back. Even now, as I write this, I feel the enemy telling me to stop. But I know who I'm fighting against and who is fighting for me. I know I've been given authority and dominion over the enemy. (Luke 10:19 NIV) And I fight back with the truth of His Word.

> *In him we have redemption through his blood, the forgiveness of sins, in accordance with the riches of grace.* (Ephesians 1:7 NIV)

When we ask the Lord into our lives, the past is redeemed, and the enemy no longer has power over us. We become new creations, and God calls us blameless, chosen, His. We can find our worth by choosing Christ – He alone is worthy!

"Riches of the World"

EMBRACE RESPECT

by Kimberly Ann Hobbs

We are all made differently by our masterful Creator - each for a specific reason and purpose. The beautiful truth is that GOD CREATED us all in His image. And He knows the purpose for which He created you.

So, regardless of how we perceive other people, we must recognize that we are all God's creations, and it is His will that we rightfully show respect to each other.

> *So, in everything do to others what you would have them do to you, for this sums up the law in the profits.* (Matthew 7:12 NIV)

As followers of Christ on our spiritual journey, we should respect all people – including other Christians and non-Christians, God, and governmental authorities.

As believers, we must be aware that God created all people in His image regardless of whether they believe in Christ or not. God tells us that the souls of individuals are of more value than all the wealth in the world. The apostle Paul tells us:

> *Follow my example, for I try to please everyone in all things, rather than putting my liberty first. I sincerely attempt to do anything I can so that others may be saved.* (1 Corinthians 10:33 TPT)

Respect is something we must learn to embrace. Showing love to all, regardless of color, nationality, opinions, or affiliations, is a form of respect. And we become an example to the lost in this world when we love our siblings in Christ. The Bible tells us in multiple scriptures that "all men will know that you are my disciples, if you love one another." (John 13:34-35 and 1 John 3:23) Love and respect go hand in hand.

As we are living examples of Christ who resides in us, the world is watching our behavior. Showing respect to everyone is an action we need to embrace to grow on our spiritual track to excellence. People may say something along the lines of "he (or she) hasn't yet earned my respect." Some say this about their adult children, and we even hear children say it about their parents. It is normal to feel this way at times, but the important truth is that this is not the attitude God wants us to have.

We can be aware of the faults of others, and we may need to discuss them, confront them, or call them out as sin when necessary, but the Bible is clear to instruct us on maintaining an attitude of respect for everyone, whoever they are.

We are all imperfect people. So, be careful not to let people's failures erode your respect for their good qualities. A way to do this is to make a conscious effort to replace any irritations you may have with them with grace. We can all find something to respect about someone if we look hard enough. Sometimes we may be required to look harder, that is all. Ask God to help you with those challenging individuals. This can be a huge feat, especially when you find difficult people you may not like along your journey. Respect them anyway, as God's creation.

If you meet someone with bad qualities, or if you struggle with things about someone that you personally dislike, do not talk behind their back or shame them. Instead, give those people over to God to deal with. Look as hard as ↗

forgiveness ↗

you can, asking God for help, and try to see His good in their design. I believe you will find at least one redeeming quality in that person. God created them. Please do not disrespect God. Remember, ask God for His help to see them through His eyes. And pray for them.

Do not dishonor someone God loves. Once I learned this, it was so much easier to love and respect everyone. I recognized who I am - a sinner who is loved and saved by God. I am thankful to God for showing me His extreme love, and because of that, I need to extend that same love and respect to others, allowing God to deal with their imperfections. We can be disappointed with the actions of others yet still respect who they are. To embrace this action word of respect, try taking delight in honoring others each day you live. Practice it.

Love each other with genuine affection and take delight in honoring each other. (Romans 12:10 NLT)

As a Christian, you are a representative of Christ in everything you say and do. May you always be a shining light to others, drawing them to the Christ inside you that you know and love. Respecting any person, whether you believe what they do or not, whether they live like you or not, whether they act like you or not, or whether they look like you or not, is the first step to an open door of communication. That communication can lead to sharing your love and the gospel message of our Savior throughout the world.

· ·

Kristina Marie Buckwald

has been married for six years to her high school sweetheart, Scott, and resides in a suburb of Cleveland, Ohio. Nothing gives Kristina more joy than being the proud surrogate "Auntie-Momma" to her niece Madison, raising her along with her brother George for the past 21 years. She is also the proud stepmom to Scotty, Stephanie, Heather, and Robby, all of whom have filled her life with so much love and purpose.

Kristina studied fine arts/jewelry design and theater in college. After college, she found her passion in the restaurant industry, and for the past 20 years, Kristina has been an accomplished and successful outside sales account executive in the industry. Kristina has a passion for all things food-related and looks forward to starting her private catering business soon.

When not working, Kristina and her husband Scott enjoy playing with their sheepadoodle named Koda, cooking, entertaining, and spending time with family and friends. Kristina is currently working on writing her autobiography and looks forward to the day soon when she can proclaim God's healing in her life.

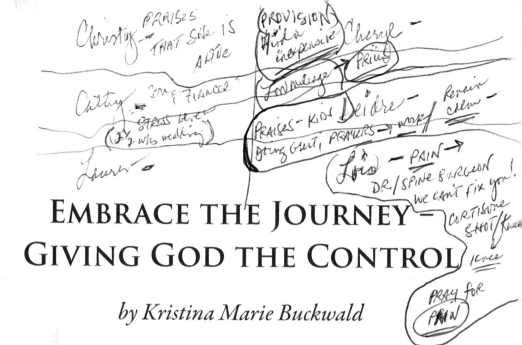

EMBRACE THE JOURNEY – GIVING GOD THE CONTROL

by Kristina Marie Buckwald

Born in the summer of 1965, I grew up in a quiet suburb outside of Cleveland. As the youngest of three, I lived surrounded by other kids in our lovely neighborhood with my two older brothers and my parents. We were an average American family who enjoyed summer cookouts; we were never without clothes, food, or family. Dad worked and Mom stayed home to care for us and always kept a tidy house.

But outside appearances kept hidden what went on behind closed doors. I'm sure most people can identify with witnessing their parents argue over dirty dishes in the sink or an unpaid bill - ordinary things that are easily resolved. But the fights my brothers and I witnessed were often over the most innocuous situations. My father's temper was volatile. We felt like we were living in a minefield, ready to detonate an explosive at any time. While my father had a large personality and explosive temper, my mother was quite the opposite. She always exuded love, gentleness and quiet grace. Although I knew my parents loved each other, their relationship had deep cracks that resulted in decades of tumultuous arguments.

I would often be startled awake from a sound sleep by arguing between my parents. Their arguments were never physical, but the verbal conflicts I witnessed created deep insecurity in me and a feeling that at any time our family could completely fall apart.

One such argument occurred when I was around eight years old. Afterward, my mother sat crying and confiding in me, asking my advice on what she should do. Not understanding the complexity of their adult argument or, quite frankly, how to provide advice without any real-life experience under my belt, I just wished all this stress away. My solution was to beg my mom to leave my dad. I told her to remove herself from the problem, and it would go away. When I realized this would likely never happen, I took on the role of protecting my mother from my father's rage and caring for her happiness and well-being. I later realized that it's not only unnatural to expect a child to process such a grown-up conversation, but that expectation also has the potential to affect every area of that child's life – including her sense of self, security, and even her health. But all I knew then was that I wanted the yelling to stop; I wanted peace, a normal family life. And I was willing to take on the role of protector to guard my sanity if that's what it took. So that is who I became.

Growing up wasn't easy. Worrying about my mom and her well-being was always at the forefront of my mind, causing me to miss out on many normal teen experiences. Thankfully, it was during my teenage years that I gave my life to the Lord. I now had a Heavenly Father who only wanted to love and guide me, yet it was difficult for me to believe that I could fully rely on God since that wasn't modeled by my earthly father. As a result, I struggled to trust God completely. I lived in constant anticipation of a phone call from my mother crying and asking for me to come to rescue her from my father's anger, stirring anxiety in me which made it difficult to cultivate healthy relationships.

In the spring of 1999, when I was 33, my brother George and his wife Jeneen had their first child, Madison Nicole. Just nine months later, Jeneen began to feel ill. One evening after rushing her to the emergency room, she was diagnosed with Acute Myelogenous Leukemia. Our world came to a crashing halt. None of us understood what this diagnosis meant, but she was admitted that night and began treatment the next day. Due to her diagnosis, she could not be around baby Madison; for risk of contracting germs. For the next seven weeks, we all pitched in, taking turns caring for Maddie. I spent hours researching Jeneen's disease and the best hope for healing. Although it didn't look good, I continued to think that I could find an answer. After the hospital she was at felt they had done all they could, it was decided to transfer Jeneen to the Cleveland Clinic.

The night before the transfer, she called me. I heard her struggle as she mustered up the courage to ask me a question. I could feel her anxiety and fear over the phone as she began to ask, "Kris, I need to ask you something...if something happens to me, will you?" And there was a long pause..... I knew exactly what she was asking, and my heart broke. There was silence as we both struggled to hold back an explosion of tears; I said, "Of course, you don't even have to ask!" I think it gave her comfort not to have to say the words, and of course, to know that I would be true to my word.

Jeneen was admitted to the clinic on a Friday. That evening, after I had spent all day with her, she called me at around 4 am. "Kris, my chest hurts; I think I'm having a heart attack." Awoken from a sound sleep, I could barely comprehend this, but I told her to press her call button for the nurse. I heard the nurse come in, and I fell back to sleep. After arriving back at the hospital Saturday morning, her doctor informed us that Jeneen had suffered a heart attack the night before. She was now in intensive care and would most likely pass soon. Somehow, I felt responsible. *Was this something I could've prevented if I had alerted someone after our call?* Jeneen, still coherent, told my brother she wanted to see me; and that I should bring paper and a pen.

As I walked to her room, I could hear my heart pounding. My beautiful Jeneen looked at me and said, "I want to have you write a letter for me to Madison." I gulped, trying to contain my tears.., "Ok, what would you like to say?" "Madison" she started, "I love you!" And that was all she could say before her tears overtook her. She looked at me and said, " I can't talk. You need to leave." I walked out of the room shaking and crying. *Dear God, why, maybe if I hadn't fallen back to sleep. If I had just called the clinic myself, she would be ok. I must've dropped the ball.*

We stayed late into the night on Saturday and all day Sunday. My family left her room Sunday night; at this point, Jeneen was nonverbal. Everyone decided to go home and get a good night's sleep as the next day promised to be a long one. Something in my spirit said, don't leave; I could not shake the feeling.

We got back to my parents' house and began to pray. Within minutes the phone rang, it was my brother. The hospital called him and said we needed to get back there as soon as possible; Jeneen was on life support and didn't have long.

Racing back to the hospital with my parents in the car, I barely remember the drive. We arrived shortly after my brother. There we were; my brother, my parents, Jeneen's beautiful mom and family and friends. We stood in a circle around her bed, held hands, and began to pray. Jeneen was disconnected from life support and one by one, we each said our goodbyes; my brother laid across her chest weeping, I couldn't speak. Jeneen wasn't passing. My Aunt, who is a nurse, said, "She isn't passing. She's waiting to hear from someone... does anyone need to tell her anything?"....It was at that moment, I spoke up, "Jeneen, I promise to you that I will step in as a mom to Madison, that I will care for her the rest of my life, and that she will know all about you and how you love her." It was at this moment that she passed, and our hearts were shattered. My sweet loving sister-in-law had left us, and in this, we were left with an enormous hole in our family and our hearts. *How could God let her die? Where is He? I should've done more! How could I let this happen??* My brother George was completely broken and lost, with a 10-month-old daughter who had no idea how her world had just changed.

The following day, I moved in with my brother to help him raise his daughter and manage his grief. I would wake up at 5 am, shower, get the baby up, feed her, make my brother lunch for work, then I would drive 40 minutes to drop Madison off at my parents while I went to work. After work, I'd pick Madison up, drive back to my brother's, clean, cook, feed the baby, and fall asleep exhausted. This routine lasted six months, I was on autopilot, assuming not only the role of mom for Madison, but also grief counselor for my brother, and all the while feeling that somehow this was ultimately my fault, I had dropped the ball. I should've done more to prevent Jeneen's death. I felt like I needed to be all things for everyone, and still protect and care for my mother. So, the responsibility continued to grow. I envisioned myself as a pack mule, and I'd just keep saying, "Sure, throw that on my back, I can carry it, no problem."

Watching Madison grow into a lovely, kind, and smart young woman has been the joy of my life! My brother eventually remarried to a wonderful lady with four children of her own. I realized life was moving quickly and if I didn't focus on finding a spouse, it would be too late for me to try to have children, so I took it upon myself to find one. Instead of looking to God to provide a spouse, I trusted the internet, which was a miserable failure. My first husband was not a Christian; we were not equally yoked, and he never understood the vow I took to my sister-in-law on her death bed. I can see now how not trusting God led me to find a man who was much like my father. Our marriage never had a chance, and after 2 ½ years of marriage, I found myself divorced and completely lost.

Several years after my divorce I was reunited with my high school boyfriend. Scott always held an incredibly special place in my heart, and I couldn't believe God had brought us back together after 30+ years. God had a plan. For the first time in my life, I felt like I was complete. I hadn't been looking for him, I wasn't in a place to even consider getting back into a relationship, but God worked out the timing and circumstances. I didn't even know what I needed, but God did. The most amazing thing about Scott is he never expects anything from me. My entire life, I've had to care for everyone. Not with Scott, he just wanted to care and take care of me. How did I get so lucky? I thanked God over and over for bringing us together.

We married in 2015, and in the spring of 2020, Scott and I were living in our beautiful home, Madison was in her last year of college, and I was at the height of my career. Then the bottom fell out with COVID-19. I couldn't work, and life was at a standstill. I felt enormous stress and even pressure in my chest, worried about what tomorrow would bring. Once again, I failed to trust God.

In March of 2020, after my father had a bad fall, I moved my parents briefly into our home so I could care for them again (as I felt only I could do). I was overwhelmed with my two 80-year-old parents living with us, managing our home, being a wife, and hoping my career wouldn't die. Then one day as I was washing dishes, I heard God speaking to me, loud and clear.

"Do you trust me?"...."Huh," I paused for a moment and thought, "Of course I trust you!", "No, do you really trust me? Because it is going to get really bad and I need you to trust me." I had no idea what God was referring to, but I assumed that at some point I was going to get COVID. I had no doubt I had just heard from God, but I kept it to myself.

Just when I thought I couldn't take anymore, my mother fell in my home, under my watch, and broke her hip. As I heard the screams coming from my kitchen, I ran in what felt like slow motion to my mom who laid on the floor. At that moment, the weight of what just happened washed over me; I thought to myself: Things are never going to be the same. *We are living in a lock-down world, she's certainly not strong enough to endure surgery, I don't know if I will ever see her again.* Once again, I assumed that this was somehow my fault. My mother, who was my best friend, and the person I spent my life-time protecting, now laid on my floor broken. How could I let this happen? I was overcome with fear. At that moment I thought, *this must be what God was referring to.*

Over the next six months, my mother went through four surgeries, lived in three different skilled nursing facilities, and continued to fall and injure her-self. I went into a spiral; I could barely breathe through all the turmoil that was happening. I kept telling my husband I couldn't take anymore; it was just too much. I felt like I wanted to die. Nothing around me was secure anymore. I couldn't count on my parents being ok, I couldn't count on my job being there, I couldn't count on our world surviving or preventing my family from getting COVID....I just couldn't. All my control was being stripped away from me, and I was completely overwhelmed. I felt like I was drowning trying to reach and grab onto a life preserver, but I just kept sinking. I recalled my favorite verse of Scripture, Proverbs 3: 5-6 (NIV) "Trust in the Lord with all your heart and lean not on your own understanding; in all your ways submit to him, and he will make your paths straight." Trust, there was that word again, Trust. God told me to trust, and I was trying, but things just contin-ued to get worse. TRUST

My chest tightened with each call I'd get from Mom's nurses. I was having trouble swallowing for a few months but didn't think much of it. During the lockdown, I found a doctor online and did a phone visit. He guessed I was probably dealing with either a hiatal hernia or an ulcer and scheduled an upper endoscopy. They removed two benign polyps and diagnosed me with a hiatal hernia. I was put on medications and continued helping and managing mom from afar. That was the worst part of it; I couldn't even be with her, the person I have spent my life protecting was alone, and my control was stripped away. I began to grow more and more tired, and the pain in my chest grew daily. I spent the next three months taking different prescription medications and going through various tests to figure out why I wasn't getting better. But my health was the least of my worries.

After fighting for another endoscopy, just a day later, I got the phone call I never thought I'd receive. It was the doctor's office, "Kristina," he said, "Can I facetime you?" What he said next took the breath out of me. "I don't know how to say this, but I have the worst possible news for you....You have esophageal cancer, and it has spread to your lymph nodes and liver. It's stage 4 and it's aggressive." (SILENCE). "WHAT?...Are you seriously telling me that I have cancer?" "Yes he said, and I'm so sorry." I fell to the floor, and all I could say was, "I've got to go"...I texted my husband, who was in the garage, "Get in here now!" I shook uncontrollably as he ran in, and I told him what just happened. "Call my brothers and my dad, let them know."

At that moment I remembered God's word at the kitchen sink, "It is going to get really bad, but I need you to trust me." Over the next ten months, I would go through 14 rounds of chemotherapy, five rounds of immunotherapy, endless doctor visits, blood draws, and scans. All of my control had been stripped away, and I knew that I was not equipped to fix this on my own. My mother was in a place where she was being well cared for, my brother had healed and moved on with his life, Madison was soon to finish college. My Father in heaven had walked us through each storm, I could now see that the control was never mine, but God worked all things together for the good, by His hand. For the first time, I relinquished my control, because I had no other choice. Proverbs 46:10 (NIV), "Be still and know that I am God," flooded my thoughts. I finally submitted my family and all my fears over to God, and

He not only has sustained me, but He also provided over and above. When I didn't even know what my needs were, He met them. My mother is now happily living in a skilled facility for people with dementia. I did nothing to orchestrate her well-being. She endured four surgeries and survived Covid and pneumonia, not by my hand, but by the power of God.

I finally became aware that throughout my entire life I thought I needed to be in control and feared that everything would fall apart if I wasn't. When everything did fall apart, I realized the key to peace and happiness is to submit control to God and fully trust in Him. It's taken me 55 years to realize this.

Now during my storm and fight, I am more at peace than I have ever been in my life. John 14:27 (NIV) "Peace I leave with you; my peace I give you. I do not give to you as the world gives. Do not let your hearts be troubled and do not be afraid." I have a God who cared enough to give me the word to trust Him! Because of His word, I can sleep at night, I know my God is in charge and that (Romans 8:28 NIV) "...in all things God works for the good of those who love him, who have been called according to his purpose." I've learned to trust, I've learned to wait, to listen, to forgive, and ultimately, I've learned to give the control over to God! I've also learned to forgive myself. None of what has happened in my life was my fault, God is the conductor and orchestrator of our lives. We cannot control the circumstances of our life, but we can trust that our Lord and Savior goes before us, He is intimately aware of our needs even before they become our needs. He is willing and able to provide for us. Let go and let God has now become my new mantra!

EMBRACE PATIENCE

by Kimberly Ann Hobbs

The saying, "Patience is a virtue," is an old cliché many are familiar with, and there is no disputing that, for Christ-followers, this cliché is accurate and is one we should strive to embrace. Patience is among the fruits of the Spirit and includes enduring discomfort without complaining, which requires us to call upon some of the other virtues, such as self-control, humility, and generosity.

Jesus is an excellent example for us in this area, as He was extremely patient with His disciples. The New Testament clearly illustrates that sometimes the disciples were stubborn, lazy, selfish, and slow to believe. How frustrating that must have been for Jesus.

Despite His wisdom and the miracles He performed in front of them, the disciples often focused only on themselves, wavering in their belief. But Jesus refused to complain over His crew of spiritually growing men; instead, He served them, displaying patience while increasing their faith until they came to an understanding. Their failures were forgiven, and the example of love that Christ laid out before them displayed Christ's patience on earth.

As you grow and embrace patience, you will learn to let go of circumstances that really irritate you. If you regularly complain over the "small stuff," I encourage you to begin to hold your tongue and then watch as your irritation minimizes. Learn to endure things that threaten to arouse an angry state in your being, and instead, give those things to God in prayer. This permits God to lift the burden of affliction from you.

Complaining to God in prayer is an outlet that can lead to patience with others. Sharing your inner feelings with God is a virtuous act. Taking your irritations and frustrations to the "Someone" who is "sovereign" can help us. He is in control of everything. Let God be the recipient of your complaint when you need to practice patience. Go to Him every time without question. God sustains the entire universe; don't you think He can manage your complaints?

For with God nothing will be impossible. (Luke 1:37 NKJV)

Sometimes patience requires waiting. In every Christian's life, there comes a time we must wait upon God. We wait for a significant desire, a fulfilled promise, or a comfort during a trial. Learning to be patient with God can teach us to be patient with others. Both can be challenging as we learn our strengths and weaknesses. The challenging work comes when we must learn to control ourselves as we wait patiently.

Patience with God involves faith to surrender final control of one's life to God. Our patience will only be as strong as our ability to overcome the desire in front of us and will increase as we surrender each aspect of our lives to God.

Pain and suffering and trial and error all teach us endurance and empathy, which helps build our patience. Even through our trials, which will include successes and failures, we can mature every day. Realize the need for patience in your life, embrace it, and then master it as you give your impatience to God through prayer.

Barb Wert

is a follower of Christ, a wife of 38 years, mother of two, and grandmother of four. Outside of technical writing, this is Barb's first publishing.

A new Florida "transplant," Barb has had the pleasure of moving to different parts of the country throughout her husband's career. With each move, God has blessed her with many special women who have helped her grow in faith and embrace the abiding joy of the Lord.

As a recent Leukemia survivor, Barb is thankful for God's truth that "to me, to live is Christ, and to die is gain." (Philippians 1:21 NIV)

Barb works remotely as a Regulatory Compliance Specialist, is an editor for *Voice of Truth* magazine, and enjoys using her time outside of work to walk, bike, crochet, play cards, and spend time with friends and family.

Victory Throughout the Journey – God Will Complete His Work

by Barb Wert

And I am certain that God, who began the good work within you, will continue His work until it is finally finished on the day when Christ Jesus returns. (Philippians 1:6 NLT)

We are all on a journey – and sometimes that journey includes storms that scar us for a lifetime. My journey began with hurt, but God had a plan, a good work He was creating in me. I love Philippians 1:6. It reminds me that although I don't feel like a completed work, that's okay because God isn't finished with me. And He promises that He WILL complete His work. That gives me victory throughout the journey, and even on the most challenging days, my faith reminds me that God is in control.

When someone asks me how I came to know the Lord, I always start with the same sentence - I had a praying grandmother. I can't say I knew my grandma well. As a child, visits with her were limited by family isolation, but memories of her quiet love remain embedded in my mind. I don't know what it was that made me so acutely aware of her love and faith. Perhaps it was her kind act of pressing a quarter into my hand at the end of a visit, which had a more significant impact than twenty-five cents should, even back then. That was one of the few acts of kindness shown to me in my childhood.

For most of my adult life, I lived halfway across the country from my grandmother. Nonetheless, my visits with her in my adult years were peaceful and sweet. While we were there, my husband would help around the house, and she would enjoy listening to our daughters talk about their lives. Grandma was "old school," however, and very private about her background, feelings, and struggles, so there's a lot I don't know about her.

But I do know what kept her strong, and I know the same thing that kept her strong had a significant impact on my life. The one thing I was sure about Grandma was that she prayed. She prayed for my sisters and me every day since the day we were each born. She prayed for our prospective and subsequent spouses since the day they came into our lives. And she prayed for our children from the moment we announced each pregnancy. If she were still alive, I know she would be praying for my grandchildren every day. Of that, I am sure.

Although I didn't always realize it, my grandmother's prayers carried me through my difficult childhood and laid a path for me to become the woman I am today. Allow me to share my journey – I'll begin with my mom.

I never understood how my mother could have been the progeny of such a gentle and Godly woman like my grandmother, but she was. I don't mean to say that my mother is a terrible person; I really can't say because I don't know. God is helping me to understand that she probably did her best at the time. But if there's such a thing as a "mom gene," I suspect my mother was born without it. She is what I would call narcissistic. I'm not a scholar, and I've never researched the term, but it seems to fit her well. Her view was myopic; life was about her. Anyone who enhanced her feeling of importance was okay. But when you gave any hint of detracting from her importance, you were no longer okay. As a mother, that meant she had no sympathy, no empathy, and no mercy for her children, and no outlook for our future. In short, she had no desire to allow her children to "be" or to help us "become" what we were called to be.

Mom's method of physical discipline wasn't out of line with what was deemed acceptable in the '60s. She mostly used a belt, with me over her knee. The first instance I remember was when I was somewhere between two and three years old. I had poured milk over my cookie, and my sister tattled. My mom told me to get over her knee and started giving me the belt. I squirmed, and she called my dad down from his attic studio. My dad got his drumstick out and beat the heck out of me. Then he asked, "Are you ready to be still for your mother now?" I was very still for the belt. No squirming allowed.

Her "practical" discipline was somewhat ridiculous, in my opinion. For example, one Halloween, when I was about five, I did something to make her mad, so she said I wasn't allowed to go out trick-or-treating with my sisters. For some reason, later in the evening she relented and said I could go down the block. What she meant was that I could go to the end of our street and back (about ten houses). I misinterpreted and went around the whole block. About an hour later, I happily walked into the house with a pretty good stash of candy. I couldn't believe my good fortune. My mother was mad because I misinterpreted what she said, and so she used my bag of candy to hand out to the rest of the kids that came to our door that night. That had a lasting impact on my five-year-old soul.

Another time, my sister and I did something to warrant being sent to bed in the middle of the afternoon. We shared a double bed at the time, and when my mother walked past the room and saw us whispering to each other in the bed, she made us stay in the bed for another hour.

If we spilled dishwasher soap, she made us wash the dishes by hand. If we didn't clean to her standard, she heaped additional cleaning on us. Stupid stuff, but it made us be on our "best behavior" all of the time. No mistakes allowed.

My mother's claim to motherhood fame came in the form of instilling shame at every opportunity. When my sister was in high school, she "took up" with a guy who worked in the factory behind our house and sneaked out of the house one evening to see him. I'm not sure how my mother found out or what the initial discipline was, but I remember that she took my sister's bed frame away and my sister had to sleep on her mattress on the floor.

In junior high school, I made it into All-State Band as a clarinetist. When the All-State announcement was made, my mother, who taught choir and music theory in the same school, told my band teacher in the presence of myself and many others that it was a fluke that I made it in because I certainly hadn't practiced enough.

My parents were both music majors in college and got married when my mother became pregnant. Back then, that's what you did, I guess. My father was no safe haven for me. I'm not sure why he was the way he was - short-tempered, unreasonable, and violent within the family home. In later years I was told that he was diagnosed with borderline personality disorder or manic-depression or something. His form of discipline included using a belt. And a drumstick. And whatever else was handy. An unexpected kick in the ribs was not unheard of. For some reason, formal beatings had to be done in the nude as I lay on my parents' bed, and from time to time ended with my father picking me up, naked, and throwing me across the room into my bed.

Impromptu beatings were handled on a situational basis. When I was in middle school, my sister's baton broke, and I was blamed for it. My father took the broken baton and beat me until I was bleeding. Then he ripped my clothes off and threw me in the bathtub to clean the blood off. He was still mad and kept dunking my head under the water and yelling while he was washing me off.

School didn't help, either. I was homely, awkward, very shy, unathletic, and I easily became the butt of everyone's jokes.

My mother left the house when I was in fourth grade, and for two long years, my sisters and I endured my father's abuse alone. Eventually, my mother remarried and settled into an apartment with her new husband and decided she wanted her children back. My father provided the perfect catalyst for her to petition the court when he swept the basement stairs with my sister's hair (he wasn't satisfied with the job she had done).

I don't mean to sound whiny or petty. These are just examples of why I grew up weighed down by shame, fear, and awkwardness. Of course, there was so much more; however, I think the gist of it is clear.

But God is faithful. Despite the difficult days of my youth, He was with me. I was the good work God had begun, and He was going to complete it. And, as I said, I had a praying grandmother who stood in the gap and whose prayers He heard.

> *Know therefore that the Lord your God is God; He is the faithful God, keeping His covenant of love to a thousand generations of those who love Him and keep His commandments.* (Deuteronomy 7:9 NIV)

I imagine my grandmother's prayers for me were prayers of thanks when I was first introduced to Christ at the age of 14. My oldest sister had been invited to church by some high school friends, and, eventually, they asked me to go with them. I heard the Gospel - that Jesus loved me just as I am, offered forgiveness for my sins, and was waiting for me with open arms. I immediately said yes. It could have been that I was starved for love, or it could have been because there were people around me who were being kind. It was probably a combination of both. If my crappy childhood contributed to my acceptance of Christ into my life, then I thank God for it. Most of all, though, I believe I was so receptive to the Gospel because my grandma had been praying for me my whole life, and God had instilled an innate faith within me.

By that point, my sisters and I lived with my mother and stepfather, and because my mother gave us a hard time about going to church, I decided it was easier to stop asking and just not go. However, there is no doubt that Grandma continued to pray on my behalf, and God was faithful. When I was 18, He put others in my life that led me to renew my commitment to Christ and begin a new journey with Him.

God has blessed me so very much since that time - more blessings than there are stars in the sky or sand on the beach. Life hasn't always been easy, but that wouldn't make for much of a journey, would it?

I can't begin to tell you how wonderful the man God provided as my husband is. He had his own dysfunctional family background, so we understood each other. We met when we were 19, and married when he was 22 and I was 21. We were terrified of being parents, but nonetheless, God gave us two daughters – both of whom are now beautiful women with beautiful hearts. And, most importantly, they are beautiful followers of Christ.

Parenthood brought to light emotional baggage that I hadn't even been aware of before. After my second daughter was born, I began having dreams about neglecting and abusing my children. I spiraled into depression and started going to counseling. That was the first time I even recognized how difficult my childhood had been. Over the next few years, buried shame and anger surfaced, taking a toll on my marriage and, unfortunately, on my children. I wasn't violent toward them; I just wasn't really there for them. Luckily, they had a super dad who carried the weight of parenting even while also working a demanding job throughout those years. And, of course, they had a praying great grandma.

We made it through that rough time, and life went on. We often moved due to my husband's job, and that kept life exciting. God used those frequent moves to help me learn how to make friends, be a friend, and be a better wife and mom. He brought many wonderful Christian women into my life who helped me to grow in wisdom and joy.

I love my kids intensely. I also love my grandkids intensely - all four! We have two handsome grandsons and two beautiful granddaughters, ranging in age from one to ten years old.

Each and every decade of my life, God has helped me to trust Him more and more. Regardless of the outcome of any burden, He has led, provided, and caused me to love Him more and thank Him constantly for His grace. And I know it all began with my grandma's prayers.

Rejoice always, pray continually, give thanks in all circumstances; for this is God's will for you in Christ Jesus. (I Thessalonians 5:16-18 NIV)

Now, at age 60, I'd like to say I've been 100% emotionally healed from the trauma of my childhood, but that isn't the case. I'm not sure God wants that to be the case, either, because He is still working out His plan. God uses everything that we go through to give us victory in our journey. For example, God uses His children to comfort those with the comfort He once comforted us. How can we do that if we forget how we felt during our trials?

> *Praise be to the God and Father of our Lord Jesus Christ, the Father of compassion and the God of all comfort, who comforts us in all our troubles, so that we can comfort those in any trouble with the comfort we ourselves receive from God.* (2 Corinthians 1:3-4 NIV)

I recently saw a picture on Facebook of a bench, with the question, "If you could sit on this bench and talk with anyone, who would it be?" It would, without a doubt, be my grandmother. I'm not sure we would actually talk because, as I explained earlier, my grandmother was very private about feelings. But I would love to put my arm around her and let her know how much I love her and what a difference her many prayers made in my life – giving me strength for the journey that I might be victorious.

The truth is, we don't turn into perfection after becoming Christian, but we can rely on God to take us through the journey as we raise families, lose people we love, fight sickness and disease, and watch our kids suffer, even into adulthood. Life is hard. It's really hard. The emotional baggage never seems to go away totally, but I'd like to think I've gone from a Samsonite extra-large suitcase to maybe a carry-on backpack. The baggage, the scars we gather on our journey, will always be there, but so will God.

Through it all, God will never leave us nor forsake us but will always be beside us, ensuring that the work He began in us will be completed. If you have accepted Jesus as your Lord and Savior, victory IS at the end of your journey. Victory is yours every step of the way when you hold onto the fact that God has a plan and a purpose for every trial, and He WILL complete His work in you.

> *Even to your old age and gray hairs I am He, I am He who will sustain you. I have made you and I will carry you; I will sustain you and I will rescue you.* (Isaiah 46:4 NIV)

EMBRACE KINDNESS

by Julie T. Jenkins

It's impossible to know what those around you are going through. That person who cut you off in traffic might be headed to the hospital to see a dying relative. The person at the checkout counter perhaps was up all night with a newborn. And that teenager who is lashing out may be dealing with abuse at home.

Proverbs 12:25 tells us, *Anxiety weighs down the heart, but a kind word cheers it up.* (NIV)

Yes, we all go through stuff, and some of that "stuff" may lead to anxiety, stress, or even a short temper. But your words of kindness have the power to turn someone's day around!

The Bible speaks in opposites quite often, as it does in the Proverb above. Biblical scholars point out that these are cases of antithesis, a specific literary device pairing opposites together to highlight the contrast. But I say that God knew us pretty well as He inspired these words! We have all had the experience of having our emotions turn on a whim. I'm guessing that you know what I'm talking about. Everything can be going along great when suddenly, the thunderstorms of life hit. But the opposite can be true, too, especially for those who are connected to God. The heavy clouds of life can suddenly break apart, allowing the sun to peek through in beautiful rays shining down. And that can happen when we are reminded of the power of God – whether that be in prayer, hearing a worship song on the radio, or...having a kind word spoken over you!

Kindness matters! God put us all here on this earth to uphold each other, encourage each other, and work and enjoy life together. But, oh, the differences we have! The way we do things often rub emotional raw spots in those around us, even in the ones we love! But God gives us the power to heal those raw spots with the salve of kindness.

Ephesians 4:32 reminds us, Be kind and compassionate to one another, forgiving each other, just as in Christ God forgave you. (NIV)

I say that this verse "reminds" us because we all KNOW the difference kindness makes! Common sense tells us that kindness can turn someone's day or attitude around – even our own. But the devil and the world try to wrap us up in our own concerns so that we "forget" that our actions and words matter. So, like a child who has to be commanded to take a nap for his own good and the good of those around him (and all the parents said, "Amen!"), as WE mature spiritually, we may need to be reminded of God's command to be kind – for our own good and the good of those around us!

You, Christian, were chosen to represent the kindness of God to a hurting world. God commands new believers to be kind. And as we grow spiritually, He keeps reminding us of this command. Leading for Christ gives us the opportunity to bless others with our kindness and to remind them, by our actions, that kindness matters. Go against the grain. Step out and embrace kindness in a world where troubles and hurts tend to make kindness an afterthought. You have God's unique power within you!

Therefore, as God's chosen people, holy and dearly loved, clothe yourselves with compassion, kindness, humility, gentleness and patience. (Colossians 3:12 NIV)

1990 23yrs

Rusanne Carole Jourdan

Rusanne Carole Jourdan is a published author, speaker and advocate for young people. She has served as a school chaplain at a public primary school since 2014.

She was born in Baton Rouge, Louisiana, representing her state in the 1984 Miss USA pageant. She's owned and operated children's clothing and women's shoes and cosmetics businesses. After receiving a degree in 1989 in Political Science at LSU, she moved to Australia. The Gold Coast, Australia, has been her home for the last twenty-two years.

"Rusty," as the Aussie's like to call her, loves to study, write, walk on the beach, go to the movies, hang out with friends and family, and experience cuisine from around the globe.

She has studied and received recognition in Pastoral Care, Christian Counselling and Bible School.

As mom of four boys, life is never boring for Rusanne. She is a full-time carer for her youngest son and is currently writing her memoir and a devotion for carers. Rusanne contributes to the Women World Leaders Voice of Truth Magazine and is a co-leader in Women World Leaders Australia.

You can contact Rusanne at rusanne.carole@gmail.com

LOIS
→ PRAYER Requests → / newbeau → pray health / LOIS → SABRINA
✓ CATHY → Aunt, EK (conversation difficult) (FRANK) goes ok! PRAYERS - E-HARMONY
✓ CHRISTY → PRAYER Son; JOB interview → Danny
✓ Deidre → KRYSTAL → BREAST CANCER (confirmation (EK) suffocating / praying
✓ CHERYL → Daughter, July 11th DRIVING TEST (PASS) license; PRAISES   JOB -

THE POTTER'S HANDS

by Rusanne Carole Jourdan

It was December 2007. I would awake each morning and lie my head down to sleep each night with the word "autism" screaming in my ears, deafening me. It had come like a thief in the night and taken my fourth son. I was lost, broken, and completely devastated. No hope.

My heart hurt. Everything hurt. The energy was completely zapped from my being. It was as if every breath my lungs tried to take ripped me apart. Continually flowing tears seem to leave permanent scars were present from the tears that continually flowed. I didn't expect to ever heal. There was no color to see. I saw everything in black and white. I could not visualize any good in the future for my son and me. I wanted to die. This was not life as I ever knew or expected it to be.

He was my youngest child of four boys. He was lost, and I could do nothing to find him.

A good mother protects her children and helps them heal when they are in need. But this was different. I did not know what to do. I cried out to God, "How could You do this to me and my son and family? I hate You! I've never done anything in my life to intentionally hurt anyone, and this is what I get!

Help me! Help me!"

I would pray the "Our Father" and "Hail Mary" prayers I learned as a young girl and cry out to God. I felt alone in the country of Australia. I had moved in 1999, away from all my family in the United States.

I felt as though I was alone in a boat with no land in sight, drowning. My son's condition, I was told, had no cure and no remedy.

What do I do?

Where do I go?

It took a full year to get any answers.

There were tests, appointment after appointment, and while I fought to get help, my whole world was falling apart.

I felt I couldn't be a mother to my other three boys. I was trying, but it was exhausting. I remember one day, after picking up the older three boys from three different schools, I pulled the car over and read something to them from a book I was reading. I explained my sorrow and guilt over not being there for them like I truly wanted to be. I'll never forget their responses. They would have been about 14, 12, and 5 years old. "Mom, we know if it were us instead of Christian, you would be there for us, fighting for answers and battling every battle to get him the best care possible." With tears rolling down all our faces, we hugged, and then someone made a joke about Christian in his baby seat, not knowing what was going on with us crying and laughing at the same time. We giggled about him possibly thinking what a crazy bunch of coconuts his family was. It was good we could still at times laugh and find humor during the hurting.

To myself, I thought how blessed I was to have three sons who were so loving and understanding, yet the guilt was still present that I just couldn't give them the time and dedication I wanted to. It would be years down the track before I would see the bigger picture and how this tragedy would bring us closer together and how it would mold them into compassionate, caring men who would be given girlfriends with a heart for children with additional needs. God was there, always there! I just couldn't see it – yet!

It had taken me over a year to get a formal diagnosis. Everyone thought I was crazy. "Boys develop slower. Just give it time." But I knew something wasn't right. Christian had his twelve-month vaccines and shortly after became very unwell and would scream uncontrollably. The substance released from his bowels was something I had never witnessed, and I had changed many a diaper! I phoned the doctor, but he said that this was normal and occurred at times. He said to give him some paracetamol, and he should be fine in a few days. He was not.

He lost all language and eye contact. I was beside myself and could not find anyone to help me. I was discouraged and hurting deeply, yet I had to hold it together for my other children. The boys' father traveled most of the year running an international business, and with all of my family in the US, I leaned on my friends. One certainly finds their true friends at such a time as this. Some stuck it out with me; others left.

I had so much hope in the pediatric specialist who finally diagnosed my son, December 13th, 2007, with classic autism. Yet, as my son walked around the edges of her room like a soldier marching the battlefield, her words gave me little hope. "I believe your son was born with this. I believe he will have to be institutionalized. He will not speak, and I hope you will be ok because I gave this same news last week to another mother, and she went home and attempted suicide."

The room stopped. My heart seemed to stop too. I tried to open my mouth, but nothing came out. Everything stopped except Christian continuing to march the perimeters of the room, oblivious to what this woman spoke over us.

I grabbed my two-year-old son, and while his father paid the bill, I heard him speaking to the doctor, "You don't know my wife, but I can tell you one thing. Our son will speak, and my wife will support him to get him to his best potential!"

I had no words. I sat in the back of the car next to my son in his baby seat. I looked at my beautiful two-year-old boy with the biggest, crystal blue eyes like the ocean water, and with tears streaming down my face, I whispered in his little ear, "Don't you worry, my love, we will get through this. Mom's never leaving you! You will speak! I don't know how we're going to do it, but we will get through this together! I will never leave you." It was God who was giving me the strength and the words to speak over my son. It would be two years to this exact date, December 13th, 2009, that I would walk into a small church in my neighborhood and meet God and realize He had been with me every step of this journey.

Things got tougher. I had to find help, which proved difficult and very costly - financially, emotionally, and mentally. There was not much support for autism in Australia that I knew of, but I tried everything I could. I found a school specializing in teaching children with autism spectrum disorder (ASD), which was wonderful until we were, a year later, asked to leave because my son was lashing out and biting the teachers.

For about six months, Christian exhibited self-injurious behavior. He bit himself and us and banged his head on walls and floors, not sleeping other than a few minutes at a time. I did not think I could go on. I never attempted taking my life, but I did think about it and how I might do it.

My twenty-year marriage ended, Christian was not improving, and my second son decided to live with his father. I had little income, and the bank was coming after my home. I was involved in a seven-year legal battle with companies and a major bank. It was hell on earth.

My mother had talked to me about going back to church. My response was, "No way." I was mad at God. I didn't want anything to do with Him. After all, He had caused this, or at least allowed this, to happen to my son.

But I know now God is a good God, and yes, nothing passes through His hands without His knowledge, but He knows the beginning from the end and the end from the beginning. The enemy came to steal and destroy my child and our lives, but God would somehow use this for good! I had to learn to abide in Him and trust Him. All my life I believed I had to be in control because there had not been many people I could trust. I eventually learned to trust my heavenly Father and surrender my life to Him. He would show me the way.

And we know that for those who love God all things work together for good. (Romans 8:28 ESV)

The Lord looks down in love, bending over heaven's balcony. God looks over all of Adam's sons and daughters, looking to see if there are any who are wise with insight - any who search for him, wanting to please him. (Psalm 53:2 TPT)

I had finally come to the end of myself and knew I needed God. My pleading led to a meeting with the One who mightily saves. It came when someone spoke Scripture to me. Hope was being restored.

"Rusanne, when you and Christian are in heaven, there will be no autism (no sickness of any kind). Jesus will wipe away every tear, and He's been collecting each tear in a bottle. He knows your hurt and your disappointment. You will have those conversations you so desire to have with your son. God will get you through this. He's got a plan, and it is a good one, for you and your son, Christian."

> *I know what I am doing. I have it all planned out – plans to take care of you, not abandon you, plans to give you the future you hope for. When you call on me, when you come and pray to me, I'll listen. When you come looking for me, you'll find me. Yes, when you get serious about finding me and want it more than anything else, I'll make sure you won't be disappointed.* (Jeremiah 29:11-14 MSG)

That Scripture touched me as nothing had before. God was speaking directly to my heart and soul. It spoke to me that God would have a good plan for me, even amid the war that seemed to be ramping up all around me. And to think that God had a good plan for my son who seldom spoke, seldom slept and hurt himself gave me a renewed hope to turn it all over to him. I could not go on by myself.

"Lord, here I am."

I decided to attend church – I had two churches in mind, and because the babysitter was on time, which was a miracle, I chose a small Uniting Church down the street from my family home. I had passed this church a thousand times, but God knew what He was doing, and His timing, as always, is perfect.

As I walked in, a young man with additional needs extended his hand to shake mine and said, "Welcome to church!" Go figure, out of all the churches I could attend a young man with additional needs welcomes me back to church. Everyone was so friendly and welcoming. That day I was invited into the Good Shepherd's house to meet and give my life to Christ. I walked up to receive communion for the first time in over twenty years, and I could not stop crying. An older lady, who would become my friend and spiritual mom, spoke to me as I apologized for crying and said, "Do not apologize, Love, for Jesus wept." It wasn't long before those people became family for my boys and me.

Years later, I realized the date and its significance. I received my son's diagnosis, what felt at the time like a death sentence, on December 13, 2007, and exactly two years later, on December 13, 2009, I was reborn in Christ and received new life.

You have granted me life and favor; and Your care has preserved my spirit. (Job 10:12 NKJV)

A thief has only one thing in mind – he wants to steal, slaughter and destroy. But I have come to give everything in abundance, more than you expect - life in its fullness until you overflow! (John 10:10 TPT)

Who is this Jesus that made such a difference in my life – taking me from suicidal thoughts to gratitude?

Who is this Son of the Most Holy God, who came to save all of humanity and give abundant life to whoever would come to Him?

Could this abundant life be for us now, not just for when we go to be with Him?

How can we possibly claim this abundant life when everything seems to be crumbling all around, like a massive earthquake, and we feel trapped under the rubble, unable to get out?

These were all questions I brought to journaling with God to understand. He speaks to us in so many ways. And the conversation with Him had begun.

The following week a lady invited me to a Bible Study. She didn't know I love to study, and I had always wanted to know more about the Bible. But God knew! And He works through people.

I had attempted to read God's Word as a young girl but gave up because it was difficult to understand. My earthly father had abandoned my sister and me when we were two years old and an infant, and I couldn't reconcile the fact that God, my Heavenly Father, wanted to be my "Abba," which means "Daddy." But I have learned that God cares for us more than any earthly father could, forgiving us and taking the punishment that we all deserve for our sin. I learned that Jesus alone could make us right with God when we accept Him in our hearts as our Lord and Savior.

The study continued every week for nine years. It was intensive, with daily reading of the Word and Scripture memorization. It became part of my life, and I fell in love with learning and teaching God's Word.

God was "setting me up" for the best adventure and journey of my life! My anger at Him melted like snow on a hot, sunny day as I began to know and spend time in the Word, getting to know Him. Healing in many areas of my heart was happening.

> *He sent out his Word and healed them and delivered them from their destructions.* (Psalm 107:20 NKJV)

I learned becoming a Christian didn't mean life would always be easy. In fact, sometimes being a Christian makes life more challenging. For example, our battle against the enemy can be most intense when the enemy sees us serving God; and we battle against our sinful nature as God prunes our imperfections, making us a greater reflection of Himself.

This process of growing and abiding in God is indeed a process - we call it sanctification. Sanctification can be joyful and painful at the same time as we take the reins off our own lives and give them to Him. It's kind of like free-falling from the top of a mountain into the mighty and capable hands of our Lord.

Uncertainty certainly remains. At times, I have been frightened about what tomorrow will bring – professionally and personally. Yet, in those times, I must remind myself to let go, to let God have the reins, knowing that I can trust Him. I may be uncertain about life, but I am certain about my God. When the Israelites crossed the Red Sea God parted the waters when they placed their feet into the water, not before, so in faith we step out but God surrounds us and the circumstances.

Beyond caring and providing for me as a single mom of a child with additional needs, God's lavish love and abounding grace have healed many areas of my life, allowing me to flourish in all that He has called me to be. He has a divine plan. We are all His creation. One thing I hold onto daily is that everything I do is for God. Everything I do for my son is for God. Nothing has helped me quite so much as reframing my thought process around this one objective. He has entrusted me with this life and my son's and all it involves, and I serve Him with His strength enabling me. It was me that needed to change.

> *But now, O Lord, you are our Father; we are the clay, and you are our potter; we are all the work of your hand.* (Isaiah 64:8 ESV)

As God's children, we can relax, rest, and trust in the capable Potter's Hands. A potter sits at the potter's wheel with the clay in front of him and uses his hands to direct the spinning force, creating a perfectly shaped vessel. Like the potter, our God, who loves us and wants only what is good for us, shapes us into valuable and usable vessels, perfectly suited for His needs. Only God knows the shaping and sculpting that is required to deepen our faith and create the masterpiece He has planned for us to be.

His molding process for us can be both exhilarating and exciting as well as scary and painful. But one thing is sure, our God is sovereign, and yielding to His Divine Plan and becoming who He made us to be even before the foundation of this world is the best adventure, we could have the privilege to take.

In Genesis 2:7, *we are told, then the Lord God formed the man of dust (clay) from the ground and breathed into his nostrils the breath of life, and the man became a living creature.* (ESV)

As Creator, God created us, formed us, and has an end design in mind for each of us – a perfect reflection of His Son, Jesus.

The potter places the ball of clay at the center of the platform, preparing to mold it into his desired, perfect shape. If the ball of clay is off-center, it will eventually form unevenly and collapse. One method that the potter uses when centering the clay is to pull it toward himself.

Like the clay on the potter's wheel, we need to be centered on Jesus so that He can shape us perfectly over time as we surrender and give Him full control.

And when He pulls us to Himself, we must submit, understanding that this is part of our molding process.

My prayer for you is that you will surrender and experience the pull towards the Father. Sometimes the toughest, most challenging, and most sorrowful experiences tempt us to pull away from the Potter's Hands. Those are the times we must be closest to Him, fully centered on Him, and in an attitude of submission as we allow ourselves to be shaped by Him. He is a good God who wants the best for His children.

I am completing this chapter on the day my son, Christian, turns sixteen years old. There were days I didn't think we'd make it. Some days remain extremely challenging, but I have learned self-care and time alone with God is what enables me to forge ahead.

My son, "Mr. C", has made amazing progress - and he speaks! Two of his favorite things to tell me are, "I love you" and "We're a good team!"

And oh, like his big brothers he wants ribs for his birthday dinner!

I'm still believing in healing for my son. None of us can fully comprehend the faithful and just plans of God on this side of eternity.

I do believe Christian came to usher Christ into my life and show and reflect Jesus and His love to others. Glory be to God!

Habakkuk 3 tells us, "Though the fig tree should not blossom, nor fruit on the vines, the produce of the olive fail and the fields yield no food, the flock be cut off from the fold and there be no herd in the stalls, yet I will rejoice in the LORD; I will take joy in the God of my salvation. God, the Lord, is my strength; he makes my feet like the deer's; he makes me tread on my high places."

My hope rests in the Lord, may yours too.

The Potter's Hand

I cannot feel anymore
I cannot understand what is going on
I cannot go on like this, Lord

Doing it all on my own
Even surrounded by people, yet lonely

What is happening, God?
In this world or in this life?

I cannot do it by myself
This I now know
I attempted to do things on my own and the outcome was never good
I need You

Surrendering
Letting go
Become pliable in your Hands

Your Hands
Powerful and Purposeful
Strong yet soft
Caressing and Caring
Directional and Developing

You knew before You placed me on Your Potter's wheel
The divine design You had planned

It takes my surrender to You

Regardless of circumstances

EMBRACE THE JOURNEY: YOUR PATH TO SPIRITUAL GROWTH

Regardless of mistakes
Regardless of delays and starting over
Regardless of trials and tears

You are the Potter
I am the clay

You are the Potter
I am Your poetry

Designed by the Designer of all things
Loved by the Lover of my soul

Even through the fire and flames of this life
As the heat of the kiln produces the masterpiece

The Master is in control
Of the watertight container of the fruits of the Spirit I desire to live by

To do the work You have planned for me

Until we are face to face
And You smile and say

Welcome home, good and faithful daughter I love

The Potter's Hands will now hold you
Now and for eternity

EMBRACE LOVE

by Kimberly Ann Hobbs

Love is a meaningful word, but it is also a word we use in many different ways every day. A well-known phrase even states, "love makes the world go around," and, after all, love does send many lives spinning into a state of utopia, but God's instruction manual on this word is far better.

Jesus is our example of true love. When we love as Jesus taught us, we seek to see others as God sees them – without fault or blemish. This type of love can only be experienced by embracing God's instruction and growing spiritually day by day. And we can be assured that as we demonstrate biblical love in our lives, others will see Jesus.

If we say we love God and want to be an example of a true Christ-follower, as many of us do, we must love one another. If we say we love God but hate others, it shows that we do not know God, for God is love.

Embracing God's love requires awareness and discipline. We cannot love while practicing racism, discrimination, or even partiality. Hate, malice, and division have no place in God's love, as these are not traits of Jesus Christ.

It is easy to show love when it is reciprocated back to us, but what if it is not? Do we then reserve our loving actions upon another? No. Despite the circumstances, we are to show love as true children of God.

However, I say into you, love your enemy, bless the one who curses you, do something wonderful for the one who hates you, and respond to the very ones who persecute you by praying for them. For that will reveal your identity as children of your heavenly Father. He is kind to all by bringing the sunrise to warm and rainfall to refresh whether a person does good or evil. (Matthew 5:44-45 TPT)

Do we live this scripture? It isn't easy to love the very ones who persecute us, but that is exactly what Jesus commands.

I have personally struggled with this. As an immature Christian, I found it difficult to be around a certain in-law. Everything he did annoyed me. Loving him was the last thing on my mind or heart. When he ate at our family gatherings, I would get up and leave the table because I could barely stand watching him eat. Irritation built up over many years. I did not like him for reasons too numerous to elaborate on, but you get the point. God had work to do on my immature heart, and He did!

As I grew in my spiritual walk and read the Word of God, every time I would see a verse that spoke of love, God would convict my heart and bring his face to my mind. I had to repent of my ill feelings toward him. My journey to loving him took time, but I eventually arrived. One thing is for certain, God will continue to convict us when we don't walk in His will. As the verse above states, "do something wonderful for the one who hates you." Well, I did that. I began to show him kindness. I reached deep inside and forgave him for all the ways he angered me. Forgiveness worked. I began to feel a love wash over me for him, and that love is here to this day. God showed me his many good qualities that I was blinded to by my anger. This man came to a relationship with Jesus, and today is a Christ-follower. He was always God's creation, even when he was ugly and irritating to me. But who am I? Am I not that same ugly sinner, saved by God's unconditional love through my Lord and Savior?

Rise above your situation, child of God. Love others without expecting anything in return. You must step forward and be the example to show love to everyone because love is an action. Jesus came to love and serve others. He showed His love in action throughout the New Testament, most importantly by His sacrifice for us. (John 3:16)

This is my commandment: Love each other in the same way I have loved you. (John 15:12 NLT)

God's love for us is the mightiest love. When we understand how God expresses His love toward us, we recognize the importance of what His Word instructs us to do for others. Love the people in your life that are difficult. Discover love in the relationships around you. Look at people through God's eyes. Put aside your own feelings towards those you do not care for, and remember your obedience is to God first. He instructs us to love. God sees your resilience and fortitude. When a person is giving you trouble, immediately release them to God and extend love and kindness as Jesus did. Watch God bring out the best in you as you obey Him. The situation will turn around. God, your heavenly Father, loves you lavishly and calls you His own. Remember, it is not about your feelings as you grow spiritually in this area, but it is all about God's instruction to you. Love one another.

Candice Daniel

is a wife to Eddie, mom to Aiden, Alec, Anderson, and Alessia, and one Angel baby. She is a Momprenuer - part owner of three very successful companies and a District Leader for her own Financial Services Business. She enjoys educating others on taking control of their finances, equipping them with the tools they need to succeed!

Candice's passion is encouraging and inspiring women to use their God-given gifts and talents to courageously walk out their calling and purpose in life. Her heart's desire is to know Him more and to share the love of Christ with the world! God is still writing her story, but she hopes to inspire others through her testimony, life trials and tribulations; to continue to have faith, and to know that with Christ all things are possible.

She is a Leader with Women World Leaders. She has volunteered with the church for many years and is a huge advocate for stopping Human Trafficking.

She enjoys spending quality time with her family and friends and connecting with others.

TRANSFORMING YOUR MIND BY LEARNING GOD'S HEART

by Candice Daniel

Do you ever wonder why we allow the voices of others to have so much influence in our lives? Why do we let their opinions dictate our actions, thoughts, and even our beliefs about ourselves?

God created us to be relational beings, and with that desire for relationship, we can be driven to work toward full acceptance by others as we long to be valued and loved. This acceptance by others can become the fuel that motivates us to pursue our passions, dreams, and purpose! But, we were each created with unique gifts, talents, and innate abilities meant to help us and guide us back to the One who created us. Because we genuinely long to be accepted and loved, sometimes we allow ourselves to get so caught up in the longing for acceptance from others that we ignore our true authentic selves. We may start altering our minds to think as others think and begin to desire the things of this world instead of focusing on who we truly are and "whose" we are. This is not something that happens all at once but happens over time, and the process to reprogram and undo those thoughts can take years and years. I personally just started this journey of renewing my mind a little over a year ago, and I can say without any doubt that this journey is far from over. As a matter of fact, my journey has just begun, but I'd love to share with you what I have learned so far.

Focusing my thoughts on God's view of me rather than the opinions of others is something I have struggled with my entire life. God created everyone uniquely – your personality, gifts, and talents are unique to only you. When we have the courage to LOVE ourselves with the same love that God had for us, we gain the ability to tap into the same power that rose Jesus from the grave, and we have the innate ability to accept others unconditionally with a love that surpasses all understanding. When we acknowledge God's love for us, there is a peace and freedom to trust God's plan for our lives.

For you to fully grasp what God has done in my life - the transformation that He has allowed to take place; I would need much more than a chapter. Numerous factors, ordained by God, contributed to the mission and quest of this journey of transforming my mind.

Like many of us, my life has been filled with trials, tribulations, people, relationships, situations, and experiences that have clouded my view of who I am. Maybe you can relate! This cloudiness led me to wholeheartedly seek God and trust Him with all I am and all I have. After all, everything I have belongs to Him anyway. Through this past year of pandemic, I have learned the most valuable lesson I have ever learned in my life. If we truly believe and have faith that God is who he says He is, then we can fully surrender in complete obedience, allowing Him to transform and renew our minds as we claim the truth that He who created us is FOR us!

When I reflect on my childhood, I recall many happy memories. But I also remember other events that had a huge part in shaping my own thoughts about myself and others. Our childhoods can have a lasting effect on how we view ourselves and the world around us. But we have a choice. We can allow those experiences, hurts, and betrayals to plague our minds, or we can choose to see them for what they are; incidents that happened to us. We are not a product of the bad choices of others. It's true that we live in a world that is full of sin, but the One who spoke the world into existence is the One who knew and knows no sin. We are children of an omnipotent, sovereign, and Holy God. He knew us before the beginning of time. He created us and knit us together in our mother's wombs. I believe that with all my heart.

> *For you created my innermost being you knit me together in my mother's womb. I praise you because I am fearfully and wonderfully made; your works are wonderful, I know that full well.* (Psalm 139:13-14 NIV)

As we walk through this transformational renewal, remembering our victories can strengthen us and help us grow into mature Christians. I have a home and a beautiful family; I have a husband who provides for us well; and I am a good, godly mom and wife. We have godly Christian friends and an amazing church family. My family is healthy, and we live a good life. But even as we remember our victories and draw strength from them, we must look at ourselves and our lives honestly and give our shortcomings to God. Do I really have all that God wants for me? Am I really living out my true purpose and the calling He has for my life? I decided to commit to walking in full obedience. To get out of my own way and allow Him to help me to begin the process of renewing my mind. Did it hurt? Yes! Was it hard? Absolutely! Is it the best decision I've ever made? Without a doubt! Why? Because it brought me even closer than ever before to the One who gave me life - Jesus! I had no idea just how much God was about to bless me. BIG TIME!

> *Let us then with confidence draw near to the throne of grace,*
> *that we may receive mercy and find grace to help in time of need.*
> (Hebrews 4:16 ESV)

Another aspect of transformational renewal is seeing things from a positive perspective. Even in our trials, there is always a nugget of joy to be gained through a lesson or opportunity for refinement. This past year was a year of many heartaches, losses, financial burdens, and pains. For many, it was also a time of seclusion, depression, sadness, and anxiety. But for me personally, it blossomed into a time of reflection, growth, and revelation. It was a year of digging deeper into the Word and drawing closer to God. So much closer than I had ever been before. It took courageous steps of faith to step out of my comfort zone and be truly vulnerable to the possibilities and opportunities that God had placed in my life. I stepped out, leaned in, and listened to the prompting of the Holy Spirit to study, write, and create. I sought out His purpose and calling He had for me and my life! I drew a line in the sand and refused to budge. I dug my feet in deep, dropped to my knees, and with wide-open arms, I cried out, "God Here I am, arms open wide, heart ready to receive and hands lifted high, I lay it all at your feet, and I give it all to you. Do what you will, and let your will be done." With my head bowed and eyes filled with tears, I surrendered all that I have, because it truly wasn't mine to give in the first place.

With everything going on in the world, I decided I needed to keep my mind filled with God's Word. I have done several Bible studies throughout the years; however, I had never actually committed fully nor finished a Bible study until this one - *Becoming Mrs.Betterhalf.* This Bible study completely changed my whole perspective and mindset on everything! It wasn't until I committed myself to consistently staying plugged in, including participating in the Zoom calls and doing the homework assigned each week, that I was able to realize just how much I had allowed the enemy to keep me from the truth of who I am and who I was called to be. I realized that prior to this intentional commitment, I had lost my joy and my passion, I had even somewhat lost myself, and I was on the verge of losing my marriage. All because I had allowed a negative, toxic mindset to occupy my mind and take root in my heart.

I started to be honest with myself and with God for the first in a long time, and I felt peace and freedom. Ultimately, I had a complete breakthrough as I began to learn so much about myself. It was as though I had been in a dark closet for a long time, and I finally was able to find the key to unlock the door and step out of the darkness and into the light. God began to reveal Himself to me in mighty ways! It challenged me to dig deep to expose some of the negative mindsets that I had allowed myself to think and entertain for so many years. I began to surround myself with nothing but positive, inspirational people and information. I began to work on me. For the first time in a very long time, I felt the presence of God. Although He had never left my side, He was more alive and relevant to me than ever before.

I saw that my marriage had not fully matured because I myself had not matured in Christ. My husband and I had always struggled with communicating effectively. My mindset and attitude came from a misguided place - that of my childhood experiences. I never had a model of a picture-perfect, healthy marriage or relationship. As a child, I witnessed a lot of anger, resentment, and unhealthy habits of communication. I believe that caused me to create a wall and a barrier in my own mind affecting my ability to trust others. And I never fully learned how to cultivate, build, and be in a healthy relationship. It wasn't until I made the decision to change my mindset and work on myself that I was able to fully admit to myself and to God where I was wrong. My husband and I had taken each other for granted and ignored issues for so long that we didn't even realize were there. I had built up resentment and anger and mistrust.

Spending time in the Bible study helped me be vulnerable and transparent with God like I had never been before. With each part of the discussions and with every question, I began to have more and more insight and revelation. God began exposing some of my innermost personal truths, truths that were only between me and Him. I had to admit some harsh realities. I had to humble myself and get out of my own way and allow Him to help me to begin the process of renewing my mind.

Allowing God to transform your mind means believing what He says about you – even if it takes some time to process what He is saying. I have been a believer since I was 13, when I committed my life to the Lord. I remember going through classes and asking the leader what he thought my spiritual gifts were because everyone has spiritual gifts, or, so I was told. I was very upset that I didn't seem to know what those gifts were. I tried hard to think about what my "special gifts" were. He assured me I had them and that maybe God had just not revealed to me yet exactly what those were. After talking for a while, we concluded that I seemed to have an overly merciful heart. What in the world did that mean? It took me a long time to understand what this meant, and I think I am still learning today just how true my leader's words were. God has repeatedly revealed this gift He has given me throughout my entire life. THIS is the truth about me that is real.

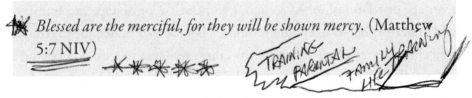

Blessed are the merciful, for they will be shown mercy. (Matthew 5:7 NIV)

Even after we put our lives in God's hands, it is tempting to look to others for permission to step out in faith and do what God has given us the ability to do. To be who God created us to be. We allow self-doubt and fear to keep us from acting on something we know God has called us to. Why do we do that? One reason is that the enemy doesn't want us to embrace our God-given journey.

He knows that if he can distract us by making us doubt the abilities and gifts that God has given us, then we will never step out in faith and act on what God called us to do. Instead, we will continue to live our lives in fear. Therefore, we will never fully fulfill God's calling on our life! And if we don't fulfill our calling, then God will never get the glory He is so worthy of! God wants the very best of you so He can bless you with the very best for you! Because He is a good, good Father. He loves you. The broken parts, the hurt, the dirt, the mess, the torn apart, the ugly, the bad, the shame, the betrayal, the stubbornness, the pridefulness, the negativity, and the hardened heart. He wants it all! He's the expert on taking all of that, all that He knows about us already. Why do we run and try to hide from the One who sees only the very best in us? There is so much beauty from all those ashes, my friend.

I recently had an illness that caused me to be hospitalized. I developed many bruises all over my body and arms from having blood drawn 2-3 three times a day. When I returned home, my son asked me, "Mom, why don't you cover up or hide your bruises? They look so bad!"

My reply was, "No, Buddy, because those bruises are a part of my story and a testimony to others that God is good, and He can use even sickness, bruises, and scars for good! I will not hide or be ashamed of them because I am not ashamed to share what He has done for me and how He has healed me!"

He said, "You're right, Mom, you're right!"

Trust Him! He will create a beautiful masterpiece from all our ashes!

As I look back over the years that have passed and at situations and opportunities where God has allowed me to influence the lives of others, I'm humbled and in awe of how He has blessed me. Despite my flaws, He has given me others to truly love. I sometimes have a difficult time reminding myself of the value I have in His eyes, but I never take for granted the ability to press through the hardest, most traumatic, and emotionally draining situations, and still find strength and faith to never give up! To cling to hope!

When we feel we are in our lowest valley, even when our physical body feels as though we cannot go on, we must remember that God is for us, and He will never forsake us. His arms are always open wide, outstretched, and just waiting for us to allow Him to transform our minds as we spend time with Him and trust His words!

God has given me an unwavering, unshakable faith and deep drive and passion to help others develop their faith in God and their belief in who He says they are! God has gifted me with the ability to see the absolute best in every single person and to love and encourage them! For years, I did not understand or utilize this gift, bowing to the lies of the enemy. But God brought me to the end of myself and revealed Himself to me as I allowed Him to renew my mind and believe what He says about me! I hope that you, too, will give your mind and your thoughts to Him, get into His Word, and get connected in a godly community, so that you can experience a deep renewing of the mind in a way that brings you freedom and deep peace so you can Embrace your God-given Journey!

Lois

They boss

* Lois — Difficult co-worker

She is her 2nd paper

* Devil is alive & well!

→ Learned from interaction

→ Praying

* * * * *

** Church online each week → Several

Chat — Swear

→ Take on screen names

Strife within the group

Embrace Humility

by Kimberly Ann Hobbs

Embracing humility is a heart attitude and not merely an outward demeanor. Throughout God's Word, He instructs us in many ways to extend meekness, lowliness, and absence of self as we live a life of obedience to our Lord.

Humility is a product for the Christian. I use myself as an example: When I came to Christ Jesus as a sinner years ago, I was required to humble myself because I had nothing to offer Christ but my ugly sin. I surrendered my lack of merit and complete inability to save myself to what Jesus did on the cross for me. I had to "die to myself" so that I could live as a new creation in Christ, and that is what I did. I exchanged my worthlessness for His infinite worth. I can now live by faith in the Son of God who gave Himself for me, as it states in Galatians 2:20. And I can now look to Jesus as a humble example. Jesus was always obedient to the Father, and as Christians, so should we. Ask yourself the question - am I willing to put aside all selfishness and submit in obedience to God and His Word? I must share that this is a daily practice for me as I strive to embrace true humility that will produce godliness, contentment, and security in my life.

God has promised to give grace to the humble, while He opposes the proud.

If you walk with the mockers you will learn to mock, but God's grace and favor flow to the meek. (Proverbs 3:34 TPT)

In the same way, the younger ones should willingly support the leadership of the elders. In every relationship, each of you must wrap around yourself the apron of a humble servant because: God resists you when you are proud but multiplies grace and favor when you are humble. (1 Peter 5:5 TPT)

We must put away our pride, confess it as sin, and trust God to help us overcome any residue that may linger in our life. Embrace God, who in His grace and for our good, teaches us to humble ourselves.

Besides Jesus, we can look up to the apostle Paul as an example of true humility. Though a great leader and one of the best advocates for the gospel, Paul saw himself as the "least of the apostles" and the "chief of sinners." (1 Timothy 1:15 and 1 Corinthians 15:9)

Jesus clearly taught us that without humility, we cannot enter the Kingdom of heaven. Having humility makes us more "child-like," meaning that we are teachable, like a little child.

When we give of ourselves in humility, with our actions following in the right intent, we can wait expectantly to see God open doors and fruit become evident in our lives.

Pray, confess your sin as it occurs, and be prompted by God to move away from pride. Embrace humility and recognize the Holy Spirit, who will help you combat the adversary who seeks to destroy those who have a humble heart. If we were strong in everything, he might just convince us we do not need humility, right? But by exercising diligence and faith, we can embrace a humble spirit. And the one who possesses true humility is the one who receives mercy and is given grace. Praise God!

· ·

Michele Hughes

Michele and her husband currently reside in Jupiter, Florida, just minutes away from the beautiful Jupiter Inlet Lighthouse & Museum. Michele's husband proposed at Marblehead Lighthouse in Ohio in 1997, and they were married the same year.

Together, they own and operate their own business, GoLifeSavers.com, which is a CPR, First Aid, and Preventive Healthcare Training Company. They also serve faithfully in church wherever God leads them, helping to inspire, encourage, empower, and equip others to find love and freedom in the one-and-only true life-*saver*, Jesus Christ.

Michele has her master's degree in education, is a #1 international best-selling author in the book *Courageous Steps of Faith,* a contributing writer and photographer in *Voice of Truth* magazine, a leader in WWL, and a retired teacher of 24 years.

She enjoys sunrises, sunsets, paddleboarding, beach walking, and capturing God's creation in photos. She loves The Father, family, friends, flowers, food, and most recently, fans!

"Give LIGHT and people will find the way." ~Ella Baker

GOD'S PERFECT PLAN

by Michele Hughes

"For I know the plans I have for you," declares the LORD, "plans to prosper you and not to harm you, plans to give you hope and a future." (Jeremiah 29:11 NIV)

You've dreamt about it. You've planned everything to a tee. All the dresses and tuxedos arrived on time, the flowers look beautiful, invitations have been sent, music selections have been made, catering choices accepted, and the photographer is ready to capture it all. And now, you are ready to walk down the aisle and live happily ever after.

Love is patient, love is kind. It does not envy, it does not boast, it is not proud. It is not rude, it is not self-seeking, it is not easily angered, it keeps no record of wrongs. Love does not delight in evil but rejoices with the truth. It always protects, always trusts, always hopes, always perseveres. (1 Cor. 13:4-7 NIV)

We had this scripture printed on ribbon bookmarks for our wedding and for those in attendance. I couldn't have been happier. It was beautiful. Away we went for a quick honeymoon that weekend and back so my husband could return to work. Do you remember the part in the vows that say, "For better or worse, in sickness and in health, till death do us part?" We all enjoy the better and health part, but what about the worse and sickness part? If you haven't experienced the latter part yet, most likely, you will.

> *So they are no longer two but one flesh. What therefore God has joined together, let man not separate.* (Matthew 19:6 NIV)

Did anyone else think that after the wedding you would continue to cuddle all weekend long, gaze into each other's eyes, say sweet things for hours, and everything would be orderly? Right after we got married, my husband started working the third shift at his factory job. Talk about a dream crusher. My new husband was working while I was in bed alone, trying to sleep. Then he would come home and wanted and needed to sleep for the day.

I was in my late 20's, teaching in an elementary school in my hometown, and had my own small house and routine. My husband moved into that house for a little while after marriage, and then we soon moved to a very large home in the same neighborhood. We were planning for a family. After several years of marriage, we were wondering why we weren't getting pregnant. Let me tell you, there is plenty of "advice" out there on this topic. We eventually went to see a fertility specialist, figuring we couldn't fix something if we did not know the problem. The doctor could not find anything medically wrong that would hinder us from getting pregnant. In fact, he told my husband he was perfect, so that made my husband feel like the visit to the doctor was well worth it!

But, on a serious note, we tried a few of the suggestions from the doctor, and we prayed about our situation, but nothing changed. We eventually decided to walk away from the concern of it and turn it over to God. We also submitted that if it were not His will for us to get pregnant, we would accept it. This actually freed me. I didn't know what the future looked like, but I knew He did. It allowed me to shift my focus. We both love children. I had a very fulfilling career teaching five-year-olds, and my husband was working at a YMCA. We still do not know why we never conceived, but we trusted God's plan for our life; He has blessed us immensely, and our infertility actually drew us closer together.

Marriage is challenging with or without children. Marriage is challenging if you have individual jobs or if you run a business together. Marriage is just challenging.

Earlier in my life, I remember thinking, *I'll never get married.* I realize now it was because I feared getting divorced. I knew it was something that could be out of my control. I also knew how much God hates it, and I didn't want to experience something so hurtful. I wondered how someone could love me enough to stay with me forever and be faithful in today's world. Now, I know that marriage can indeed be a challenge, but if both spouses have a personal relationship with Christ, it is quite possible to have a healthy marriage that defies the world's odds. I now look at what I would have missed out on because of fear and doubt, and I am grateful for how God has blessed me with this *gift* of marriage. It helps me to be less selfish and understand unconditional love.

Like most couples, we entered marriage with individual goals and visions and knew we needed to figure out balance, including how to journey and set goals together. God gave us marriage to enjoy and display the gospel. In Genesis, we read, *The Lord God said, "It is not good for the man to be alone. I will make a helper suitable for him."* (Genesis 2:18 NIV), and *For this reason a man will leave his father and mother and will be united to his wife, and they will become one flesh.* (Genesis 2:24 NIV) Marriage is two imperfect people covenanting their lives together, for better or worse, in sickness and in health, until death parts them. This is a beautiful picture of Jesus Christ (the groom) and His never-ending *love* for the church (the bride.)

As I grew in my relationship with Christ, He taught me what marriage is about. It's about *Him.* The purpose of marriage is to point others to this important relationship: Jesus and the church/husband and wife. God's blueprint is for Christ and the church to become one.

> *A new commandment I give to you, that you love one another; just as I have loved you, you are to love one another.* (John 13:34 NIV)

As I share about marriage, and I specifically use my marriage as an example, I am writing from my point of view with my husband's approval. My husband spent his childhood summer vacations around Sandusky, Ohio, and frequently visited Cedar Point amusement park. When he proposed at the Marblehead Lighthouse, we could look across the lake at the rides. This vision came to mind as I was thinking about this chapter. Marriage is like a roller coaster: You wait around in anticipation until it's your turn to get on. Some people back out at the last minute. You put on the ring and strap yourself in. The wedding is the first big hill that clicks very slowly along until it reaches the top, then the honeymoon, the climax, and then... hold on tight! You may experience some bumps along the way and some ups and downs. Some thrills. Some twists and screams. Some will literally vomit. There may be some dark tunnels. Some will feel like their world has been turned upside down. There may be some sudden stops. Some will throw their hands up. Others will smile and laugh and close their eyes. But no matter where the ride takes you, buckle up. Hold on tight! Stay on track. Don't get off before the ride comes to a complete stop. When it's over, you may realize you enjoyed it.

> *For the LORD God of Israel says That He hates divorce, For it covers one's garment with violence. Says the LORD of hosts. Therefore take heed to your spirit, That you do not deal treacherously.* (Malachi 2:16 NKJV)

Satan wants nothing more than to make us think our marriage is so bad that we should divorce. So, what do we do when those bad times strike, and how do we handle them? Unfortunately, when bad times came, my husband and I often got angry and exhibited bad tempers, sometimes leaving the room or even walking out the door. Other times, we used the silent treatment on each other.

> *Though one may be overpowered, two can defend themselves. A cord of three strands is not quickly broken.* (Eccl 4:12 NIV)

When it comes to marriage, it comes down to this: **What would Jesus do?**

One of the first things Jesus would do is to communicate clearly.

At my bridal shower, I received plenty of advice about the importance of communication. Although I took mental notes, I didn't realize how difficult it could be to talk openly or honestly with my spouse. I found it scary to bring up issues early on because I was unsure how my husband would respond. I feared my communication would make things worse. Sometimes it did, and I was tempted to quit trying to improve our marriage. But unspoken anger and resentment can build up over time, and when there aren't little ears and eyes around, as in our case, we found it easier to show our ugly side. As we've grown spiritually, we have found that when we pray about a situation *first,* God guides our words and prepares the listener's heart.

It's easy to forget that *listening* is part of communication. Listening must be a priority for both spouses. My husband came into our marriage with hearing loss in one ear, and as we age, it continues to weaken. We have talked with several couples with hearing aids, and they shared both the challenges and the improvements that hearing aids can offer. These conversations motivated my husband to eventually take the plunge, get tested and fitted for hearing aids, and purchase the best on the market. Hearing is a practical and physical aspect of listening.

In addition to communicating clearly, I believe Jesus would be acutely aware and appreciative of the other individual in the covenant relationship.

Sometimes the qualities we once admired in our spouse can slowly turn into behaviors that annoy us. My husband has such a strong work ethic that I know I will never starve. But on the other hand, I often find myself eating alone because he is tending to work. When I find myself frustrated at this quality I once admired, I intentionally remind myself to appreciate the positive aspect of his personality.

Often it's true that opposites attract - we are drawn to those who are different from us. That is certainly the case in my marriage. For example, he is the spender, and I'm the saver. He is the talker, and I'm the listener. He likes to ignore things, and I like to address them. He likes administration, and I like doing. He likes to have everything out where he can see it, and I like to have it all put away in its place. He prefers to drive like a racecar driver, and I like to see the sights along the way and smell the roses. Intentionally appreciating his views and agreeing to disagree are two ways we have successfully handled seeing the world from different angles. Prayer and patience are essential. If I can speak transparently, appreciating each other's differences is something my husband and I work on daily. And we never discount that we are *similar* in the ways that *matter.* For example, Christ is Lord of our lives. We believe in healthy spirit, mind, and body. We are friends and not just lovers.

Besides being intentionally aware of the other spouse, in marriage, Jesus also calls us to respect each other.

> *However, each one of you also must love his wife as he loves himself, and the wife must respect her husband.* (Eph. 5:33 NIV)

Throughout my marriage, I often found myself getting frustrated, thinking how much better our relationship could be and the blessing we were missing when only one of us wanted to work on our relationship. (Jesus probably thought the same thing about me once or twice.) But, looking more closely, I realize my husband also knows the importance of working on our marriage and is willing to put in the time and effort. But in reality, he is often busy with his responsibilities. I choose to respect that he is doing his best in the situation. Remember the hearing aids? As it turns out, my husband rarely wears them, which is a frustration for me. So I turn it over to God, asking Him to help us work through this and to help me respect the psychological or emotional ramifications that this situation may be causing my husband. This has allowed me to grow in patience and acceptance.

Respecting someone includes giving him or her your full attention. This brings me to the "third person" in many marriages today, including mine - the cell phone. The cell phone, as we have all discovered, is a blessing and a curse. It allows us to always be connected to work and social media, but it often disconnects us from those who are physically in our presence. When handled intentionally, the phone can mean spending more time together as a couple. When mishandled, it can lead to a lack of respect for your partner. We learned that the key is to find out what works for our marriage. We needed to find balance and community and allow Jesus to lead us, trusting *what Jesus would do.*

And now these three remain: faith, hope, and love. But the greatest of these is love. (1 Cor. 13:13 NIV)

We believe God blessed our marriage and joined the two of us together and, as we learn more about God's love, we learn how to love each other better.

1 Peter 4:8 NIV says, *Above all, love each other deeply, because love covers a multitude of sins.*

After five houses, three states, and a few job changes, my husband and I now own and operate our own business in Florida and throughout the United States. We work together, work out together, sleep together, travel together, serve together, and lead groups at church together. Some people have told us, "We would kill each other if we spent that much time together!" Because we were friends first, we actually enjoy spending so much time together.

Marriage life is always changing, and we need to keep adapting. When spending as much time together as we do, it can be easy to be functional irritators. We have to remind ourselves constantly that we are not the enemy. And, just when I think we've got this marriage thing down, another curve appears. We've read the books, attended the classes and marriage conferences, and still have conflict. Why? Because conflict is inevitable. We are imperfect sinners. Why are we still together? Because we are getting better at forgiving and turning toward Jesus, honoring our commitment, and remembering to love like Jesus.

Be kind to one another, tender hearted, forgiving one another, as God in Christ forgave you. (Eph. 4:32 NIV)

We have found that when we put God at the center of our marriage, He is faithful to guide us on this *journey*. We pray out loud together daily. We are committed and continue to invest in our marriage and date each other. As a child, I learned this quote: "Make a decision and learn to manage it." God has used this to protect me in several situations. During one of our low points, I remember saying, "We can either live forever happily or forever miserably. I'm not leaving, so the choice is yours." But really, the choice is *ours*.

God made woman to be a helpmate for man. As a wife, I haven't always lived up to this role; but as I strive for my own *spiritual growth,* our marriage improves. As the head of our house, my husband has a huge responsibility. I need to cut him some slack and be that helpmate he needs. Sure, at times he might act like he doesn't need me, but I know he does, and I need him. That's the way God designed it.

God desires that people on earth live out the redemptive plan. Our marriage is a message that people are watching us model. So, we really should bring glory to God, showing people the gospel message through our marriage. I don't know about you, but that speaks to *me* and helps hold me accountable.

Marriage matters! Our *worst day* together is better than a *good day* apart. It's easier to love during the good times, but we must recognize we grow in love in the bad times. Often what frustrates us, we also admire. No one can make me angrier, and no one can bring me more happiness. Love is worth fighting for. We are better together. Time on earth is short. I regret being too serious and wanting things to be "perfect" and wasting good times. If I could start over or change anything, it would be to laugh more and pray more. One day, most likely, one of us will pass, and the other will be left behind. What will they remember? I don't want to be left with regrets.

As I reflect on my relationship with Christ, and as I spend more time in His Word, I pray that I will look more and more like my Savior and less like myself. We are called to reflect Christ rather than hide Christ. Lord, forgive me of the times I have not allowed Christ to be seen.

> *And we all, who with unveiled faces contemplate the Lord's glory, are being transformed into His image with ever-increasing glory, which comes from the Lord, who is the Spirit.* (2 Cor. 3:18 NIV)

To the one who is young, single, widowed, abandoned, divorced, or the one ready to throw in the towel, today is a new day. *Embrace your journey.* Draw closer to God and know everything is going to be all right in the end if you have a personal relationship with Jesus. One day, we WILL have the *perfect* marriage. But, until the end, let's *embrace the journey through spiritual growth.*

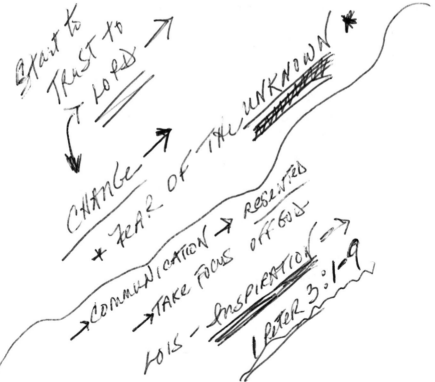

→ ETERNAL DEPOSITS

IMITATORS of GOD!

DISRESPECT? → BEAT & SPIT → Jesus

FOCUS on Jesus

UNDERSTANDING THAT

SATAN → WORKING

HARD →

EMBRACE PRAYER

by Julie T. Jenkins

Prayer should be our "go-to" in life. Are you unsure about something? Pray and ask God for His wisdom and guidance! Are you worried or feeling fearful? Go to God, request His presence and His peace! Are you joyful? I can't think of anyone who would love to celebrate with you more than God!

The Bible is full of examples of and teachings on prayer, but if there is one take-away I want you to learn about prayer today, it's that God WANTS to spend time with YOU! He made you for His joy, and He thinks you are pretty darn cool. I just got a new puppy, and it is thrilling when he comes running to me! And YOU have the power to bring God joy way beyond what my puppy brings me! That's why He instructs us...

Come to me, all you who are weary and burdened, and I will give you rest. (Matthew 11:28 NIV)

Do not be anxious about anything, but in every situation, by prayer and petition, with thanksgiving, present your requests to God. And the peace of God, which transcends all understanding, will guard your hearts and your minds in Christ Jesus. (Philippians 4:6-7 NIV)

> *Ask and it will be given to you; seek and you will find; knock and the door will be opened to you.* (Matthew 7:7 NIV)

And while we bring God joy by running to Him, we can be assured that God will bring us joy, too. While I have experienced God's joy when going to Him in prayer, there are honestly also moments when I don't *want* to go to God. If I were to dissect those times, I know I would clearly see that they followed a period of sin in my life. This is natural. After Adam and Eve sinned, they hid from God in the garden. (Gen 3:8) And Isaiah tells us point-blank that our sins separate us from God. (Isaiah 59:2)

I am not proud to share with you that there have been days when I have gotten so frustrated with my kids and have yelled at them unmercifully. And, when I tear myself away – and usually go for a walk – God is the last person I want to talk to. I'm embarrassed, ashamed, and guilt-ridden.

It's in those moments that I have to remind myself that God knows every single one of my flaws, and He wants me to go to Him anyway. We are all sinful, and like satellite reception that is interrupted due to a storm, our sin will interrupt our communication with God. But God hasn't gone anywhere! He is still there, waiting for us to turn to Him in repentant prayer so that He can restore our full communication with Him.

God should always be your go-to. Your best friend. Your confidante. Jesus' death tore the veil that separated humanity from God's presence. As a result, we can go to Him anytime, anywhere. You don't need a designated location, the right prayer formula, or specific words. God is just waiting to have a conversation with you! Abide in Him and allow Him to strengthen you and celebrate with you!

Truly my soul finds rest in God;
my salvation comes from Him.
Truly he is my rock and my salvation;
he is my fortress, I will not be shaken.
(Psalm 62:1-2 NIV)

(Prayer Requests)   (7/27/2022)
. . . .

Maureen - Health →
            DETAILS
            knee surgeon; DVT; Blood Clot →
Lois - HEALTH →   TIRED; WEAK; Procedure - monday
            (PRAYING FOR SABRINA) ← CHEMICAL STRESS TEST
                          PROVISION → GOD'S
                          BLESSING

• CATHY = JOB → OPPTY → →→ COMPLETE INTERVIEW (SUNDAY)
         PRAYING FOR SPARK INTERVIEW; GOD OPPTY TO TRANSITION
         PRAYING FOR CLARITY; NAIL JOB

• CHRISTY - PRAYING; CLARITY; GUARD AGAINST POSITIVE
                              FOOLISH DECISIONS; SITUATION

DIERDRE - BUSY; w/WORK - OT; STEP-DAD COVID PNEUMONIA,

CHERYL -

LAUREN - (GOD HAS PLAN) MARGEAUX

230   EMBRACE THE JOURNEY: YOUR PATH TO SPIRITUAL GROWTH

Lois Daley

Lois Daley, the mother of three, has walked with Jesus for over 50 years. She is a Bible teacher, speaker, published author, and prayer fanatic who holds academic degrees in aviation and business and has attended Bible college.

The firstborn daughter of two powerfully effective Bible scholars and teachers, she was saturated in Bible knowledge early. She has led multiple ministries, including women's ministry, prayer team, choir, and children's church. Presently she is a Prayer Team Leader for both her church and Women World Leaders.

Lois has written Bible studies and poetry and is a contributing author in *Tears to Triumph* and *Courage Steps of Faith.* She spends a lot of time on her knees and cherishes adding you, her reader, to her list for daily intercession.

Her passions include prayer, music, gardening, and watching football. In the fall, you will often find her adorned from head to toe in University of Miami's Hurricane garb.

Her life verse, "For to me to live is Christ, and to die is gain," can be seen in her tender, unbashful conversations, prayer, and singing about God.

Living for Christ is eternally priceless

Roman 8:18
Phil. 1:21

FORGIVENESS

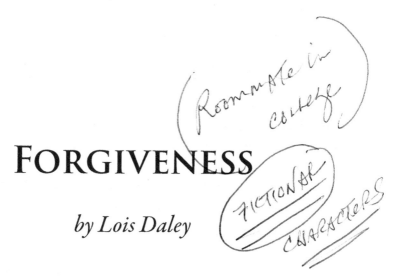

by Lois Daley

"Hurt people, hurt people" is an aphorism often attributed to Rabbi Yehuda Berg and Rick Warren, evangelist pastor, but research shows it dating back to 1959 when quoted by Charles Eads. This popular aphorism is used by many to explain and excuse bullies, recess fighters, prison brawls, and various kinds of abusers.

My parents and extended family taught me to be kind to others. Ephesians 4:32 (KJV), says *Be ye kind one to another, tenderhearted, forgiving one another.* This was a verse drilled into my psyche from a very young age. As a child, whenever there was a hint of unkindness in our home, my brother and/or I had to write Ephesians 4:32 out many times.

I grew up in an environment where my older cousins lived next door. I was next to last on the pecking order of age, and so I knew that respect was due to the older cousins. This was the norm in the Baby Boomer and before generations where I lived. Most of the time, we played peacefully with my younger brother and the two cousins a few years senior to me. The others were older and lived their lives away from the imaginary supermarket, church, school, and whatever else the four of us would conjure up in a big blue dollhouse that my uncle had built in my grandfather's backyard. Life was good throughout my school years. I had the love of my mother and father in our house and the joy of grandparents, aunts, uncles, cousins, and other extended family who lived in the great house next door. Whenever I was not at home playing with my family, I was at school, piano lessons, church, or other activities that my parents felt were necessary for an upcoming pastor's wife. (That information I found out later in life. So contrary to my vision and plans.)

After high school, my mother decided that I needed to experience the world of employment, but not without her input and control. Being a well-known businesswoman with many contacts and associates, she took me to one of her friend's companies to work. A few months into that job, Mom changed her mind (for reasons I do not know to this day) and placed me at another job where a very close friend and church comrade was in senior management. Personally, the move for me was very positive. The new job was in a very large financial company in the heart of the city; hence, I would have the opportunity to experience a new facet of adulthood.

Little did I know that the overprotected existence that I had during my formative years and up to that point would open situations that would test my moral fortitude and my spiritual resolve. This was the real world, a place where some people cussed, did not attend church, and even those who attended church had a different interpretation of God's ways and practices than what I was taught. For the first time in my life, purity and righteousness were jeered at, open sexual overtures were the norm, and off-colored jokes were laughed at with belly rolling cheers. This was the workplace pre-twenty-first century and the Me Too movement.

I enjoyed the daily task that I was employed to do. As personalities got familiar, I chose to associate with those who were not only close in age but who seemed decent, and with those whom I evaluated had some sense of godliness and were fit to meet my pastoral parents, if need be.

The delight of knowing new people gave my heart joy, but as time went on, many folks discovered some of my weaknesses. "Familiarity breeds contempt," is another popular phrase. I was a major people pleaser and did not like to hurt another person's feelings. I was teased and called "bird legs" because I was very thin - at eighteen years old, size 00 skirts would have to be altered to stay steady on my waist. And some people scoffed at me because of my commitment to Jesus Christ. I would decline going to some of the places of pleasure that many of my coworkers frequented. After a few months, however, I had grown accustomed to the jokes and conversations, and I clung closer to the few friends that I had made.

The painful moments came when those who called themselves Christians would join in playing unkind pranks on me when I went to lunch hour prayer sessions at a church a few blocks away. Those pranks ranged from hiding my lunch in dusty filing cabinets to telling lies on or to me. Coworkers regularly shared congratulatory laughs at their folly and seemed so satisfied to have pulled one over on me again. Many times I hid the hurt, and sometimes I even laughed it off to hide my pain. One particular lady seemed to be the head of those pranks. Occasionally, my friend Char would ask me why I put up with being treated so poorly. I usually did not have an answer for her.

Although I was familiar with my Bible passages, especially the New Testament, I did not apply Scriptures such as 1 Peter 4:16 (ESV): *Yet if anyone suffers as a Christian, let him not be ashamed, but let him glorify God in that name* or Matt 5:11-12 (ESV), which I could quote from memory, *Blessed are you when others revile you and persecute you and utter all kinds of evil against you falsely on my account. Rejoice and be glad, for your reward is great in heaven, for so they persecuted the prophets who were before you.* I suppose I prioritized covering up the hurt so much that I did not take the time to surrender my teenage problems to God.

After three years working at the financial firm, I decided to go to college, so I quit my job. I was elated. Not only was I leaving home, but this was my decision. I was exercising my adulthood rights. My mother was not too pleased, as I would be very far away from her. In addition, there was a boy that used to live close by with whom I had started a long-distance relationship, and the university was closer to his residence.

Helen, one of my coworkers, was forging the same path and attending the same university. In my naivety, I accepted the invitation to be her roommate. I did not think of the many times she had hurt me at the job. My mind was clouded by my new freedom, the degrees that I would be pursuing, the pride my parents would have at the end of my studies, and of course, the short distance to hop on the expressway to see the man I was in love with.

It did not take but a few weeks for the novelty of my new living situation to wear off. Helen would criticize my clothes, my church, my man, and anything else she could find. Together, we had made travel arrangements to and from school, but she would often amend them without informing me. As a result, I would have to walk a long distance alone in the dark to get the city bus to attend school and reverse the process to return home. Sometimes my nose was so cold and frostbit that I thought it would fall off. Still, I remained the sucker I was at that time. I would try to appease her and invite her on many of my dates. Wayne, my boyfriend, would ask me why we had to take her with us, but I always felt pity that she was alone in the apartment. Plus, I told him that my family used to say that we should never leave anyone out. Kindness was embedded in my DNA, and there was no way around that. However, when I befriended anyone at school, Helen would sabotage my friendship, so I stayed alone most times.

The core of my heart began tearing when she told mutual friends at the university stories about me that were not true. The stress and gossip ate at me.

Still, I did not say anything. I would swallow the abuse day after day. There were times I came home and I could not get in because the night lock was on in the afternoon.

One day my Mom and Dad visited. It was just before the summer break. My family was on their way to one of their European excursions. My mother pleaded with me to come along with them. I had 'been there and done that' as a child and did not want to be under my mother's scrutiny anymore. So, I declined. Nevertheless, in Mom's wisdom, she figured out what was happening to me based on the way Helen bragged about her own diligence and put me down, implying that I was inattentive to excellence in academics. Fortunately, my grades showed otherwise. Mother insisted that "all work and no play made Jack a dull boy," and she offered to pay for me to go on vacation anywhere I wanted to. I leaped at her offer and was only too happy to choose my vacation destination and visit some of my cousins. I would get a break from the emotional blows.

However, when I returned for the fall semester, it was as though the abuse stewed and simmered in my absence, just waiting on my return. I cried a lot that semester. Often I would console myself with singing or taking a walk through the neighborhood, admiring the different trees and flowers as salty teardrops trickled down my cheeks. Another escape method I chose was to load my school schedule with extra credits, which I got approved by my academic advisor. And sometimes I would stay at the school library for fear of going home. Still, I did not tell anyone of the emotional pain I was feeling.

The cruel occurrences lessened, and that was a relief for me, until the day Helen decided to drive Wayne's precious car. He had come to visit me and she saw his keys on the little table and just picked them up. Even I had never sat in the driver's seat, much less attempted to drive his car. At that point, my feelings were totally crushed. I had had enough.

My go-to behavior became silence.

That semester I spent most of my time at school. My diet consisted of vending machine foods and overpriced cafeteria lunches. Soon I developed an ulcer in my stomach. On weekends, I would ask Wayne to come for me; I preferred to tolerate his family quirks over the torture I was subjected to Mondays through Fridays. Whenever he could not come, I would go over to an older couple's home who were my aunt's friends.

That Thanksgiving break, I went with my boyfriend's family and friends on a trip. The following Sunday, when he brought me to my apartment, I refused to come out of the car. Overwhelmed, angry, hurt, and anticipating more pain, I sunk my derriere in my seat as I began crying and screaming.

"I can't go! I'm not going!" I yelled as I clung tightly to the car door, reluctant to open it.

He, too, had his college to attend the next morning, sixty miles away. Wayne kept pleading for me to get out. I kept creaming. A pain ballooned in my heart. There could be no way for me bare any more emotional battering.

Suddenly an idea came to mind. An old family childhood friend and her parents lived not too far. I told Wayne to drive over to their house. I planned to explain my situation and ask if I could rent a room from them. Fortunately, upon hearing a short version of my story, they agreed to allow me to live with them.

Life improved for me, but the heartache remained. I avoided Helen at school. Many times, if I saw her, I would take an alternate path to class, even if it were a longer route and it meant arriving to class late. When that semester was over, I had enough credits to graduate. I felt relieved that I would never have to see her again.

For over a year, my experiences haunted me. I developed a hatred for Helen. I even detested my weakness and the fact that I could not stand up for myself. I was afraid to make new friends.

Over and over, Ephesians 4:32 replayed in my head. I could not forgive someone who was so bent on destroying my reputation and my life, someone whom I had embraced as a friend yet repeatedly betrayed me.

Eventually, I came to grips with my heart.

The end of the Ephesians 4:32 (KJV) says *as Christ has forgiven you.*

How did Christ forgive me?

He was mocked, beaten, betrayed by His close friends and other humans that He made, yet He still died on The Cross to pay the price for the sin of all mankind, including me. He did not die for His own sins, because He never sinned. I personalized that. He was forgiving me and reconciling my broken relationship with God. He gave me eternal, perfect life so that one day I will spend my forever with Him.

I mulled over that concept for days, then one day, I sat down with tears streaming down my cheeks and asked God to free me from the shackles of unforgiveness to Helen. It was a solemn surrender to a difficult task, but I had confidence that God would strengthen and help me through the process. Peace and liberation replaced the pain of the hurts. *Hatred stirs up strife, but love covers all offenses.* (Proverbs 10:12 ESV)

For years I did not see Helen. Our paths did not cross until one day I had the opportunity to see her. But I still did everything to avoid facing her. I knew I had forgiven her, but my pride held me back from approaching her. Years passed again. Then The Lord gave me another chance to do the right thing. I was made privy of a function that she would be attending. I would have to be intentional and go to the function. I followed God's leading and strength and went. I boldly went up to her. We embraced tightly, without speaking. Somehow there was more said in that moment than words could ever utter. Since then, we have had long conversations, and a different relationship started.

I thank God that He has released me from unforgiveness and has given me the power to be at peace with all. Romans 12:18-19, 21 (ESV) says *If possible, so far as it depends on you, live peaceably with all. Beloved, never avenge yourselves, but leave it to the wrath of God, for it is written, "Vengeance is mine, I will repay, says the Lord." ...Do not be overcome by evil, but overcome evil with good.*

Forgiving another person may not be easy, but with God, nothing is impossible.

EMBRACE FORGIVENESS

by Kimberly Ann Hobbs

When we embrace forgiveness, we understand the importance of releasing the hold of hurt, disappointment, and discouragement.

Forgiveness has nothing to do with the person who offended us or even the offense itself – it has only to do with us and how we allow God to work in us. When Jesus is our partner and the Holy Spirit leads us, God alone brings us to grace and mercy.

We live in an imperfect world with imperfect people. Feeling disappointed, hurt, or betrayed, whether by an intentional or unintentional act, are all part of the human experience. It has taken me years to learn and recognize forgiveness and appreciate how powerfully it impacts every facet of my life and the lives of those around me - spiritually, physically, emotionally, and mentally.

What is God's teaching regarding forgiveness? We are called to forgive as we have been forgiven. It is not a choice; it is a command.

> *But instead, be kind and affectionate toward one another. Has God graciously forgiven you? Then graciously forgive one another in the depths of Christ's love.* (Ephesians 4:32 TPT)

As we grow spiritually, we grasp true forgiveness and the fact that it was granted to us through Jesus Christ. Forgiving others is an opportunity to glorify God out of the abundance of the forgiveness we have already received.

Do you realize we received forgiveness at a cost? The cost was Jesus' life! So how can we not be fully devoted to Him and be obedient to what He says in Ephesians 4:32? Full devotion includes obedience. And ongoingly offering forgiveness to others is a part of that obedience.

> *God does not call us to do anything He has not equipped us to do. He gives us generous grace so we can use it for our good.* (2 Peter 1:3)

Choosing to forgive releases the offense and allows us to do what God wills. Please do not allow bitterness and resentment to grow in unforgiveness. Choosing unforgiveness will prevent your heart from healing.

True freedom comes as you learn to forgive, unshackling you from past offenses and hurts someone else may have caused, allowing you to move forward in freeing release.

Let go and let God. Give him the offense, so it does not ZAP you of energy needed to live in the present, and then move forward from the offense.

Forgiveness is a skill in this broken world, and I find the longer I live, the more I need to rely on this tool to allow my relationships to thrive. I fall short every day, and God forgives me, and, thankfully, I now extend forgiveness myself, inviting God's grace and goodness to thrive around me. It is important to leave a legacy of godliness in our families. Forgiveness is evidence of unconditional love and compassion in our relationships, something we must work on every day. Practicing forgiveness will allow us to grow into the spiritual giants God intended us to be.

Besides harming your earthly relationships, unforgiveness left inside your heart will also harm the relationship you have with God. Please do not interrupt your fellowship with God by possessing an unforgiving spirit. We are to confess all known sins to God, including unforgiveness, allowing our spiritual lives to soar to new levels. Through forgiveness, we can thrive on the freedom of relief and release into a newness of life, a new path, a path to spiritual growth. Draw close to God, asking first for forgiveness for yourself and then practicing the forgiveness of others, just as God has forgiven you. Then you will walk your path unencumbered, and you will be a witness to others of the freedom that forgiveness brings.

Claire Ellen Portmann

is wife to Brian, mama to Kimberly, daughter to Janet, and little sister to Larry. With a heart on fire for Jesus, she is running the race for the glory of the Kingdom of God.

For over a decade, Claire and Brian have worked breeding and raising English Cream Golden Retrievers for families all over the United States. In their hearts, they knew they wanted to leave a legacy showcasing God's faithfulness to them, so with that in mind, they took what God had blessed them with and trained their first therapy dog, Finn. Finn and the rest of their growing team now go out to bring the Gospel of Jesus Christ to the lost and broken of this world. This year they are starting a clothing line called "The White Dog," which will feature their precious English Cream Golden Retrievers.

Claire is a #1 bestselling author, having written in *Tears to Triumph* and *Courageous Steps of Faith.*

She loves spending time with her church family and lives in Jupiter, Florida.

A RESURRECTED HEART

by Claire Ellen Portmann

Sometimes to grow as a Christian, we first need to heal from our past. Both healing and growth are not for the faint of heart, but take intentionality and work. And to truly embrace this journey, it certainly helps when we allow other Christians to speak into our lives and to hold the flashlight as we walk along the path.

I have a dear friend Amber, who knew I was trying to grow as a Christian. One night as we sat watching puppies in my master bathroom - my husband Brian and I breed English Cream Golden Retrievers – we discussed the concept of Christian growth, and God turned our conversation to one of inner healing. Amber, knowing my background, suggested that my next step of spiritual growth should be one of deep inner healing. She suggested that I should work with a spiritual director she knew named Deirdre.

Amber and her husband run a nonprofit called "Everyday Mission," which is a voluntary, intentional community of missions and microchurches. They are selfless, wonderful, loving people who are making a difference for the Kingdom of God, and I simply adore them. And I trust them because of the spiritual fruit they bear. It's easy for someone to say that they are connected to the

Holy Spirit and walk in His leading, but when aligning ourselves with other Christians, it is important that we see fruit produced by that connection with the Spirit.

> *Yes, just as you can identify a tree by its fruit, so you can identify people by their actions.* (Matthew 7:20 NLT)

Trusting Amber, I made some phone calls and appointments and began speaking with Deirdre once a week. Together, we walked through the process of inner healing. Deirdre lives in Chicago, and I live in Florida; despite the distance between us and the restraints of the COVID outbreak, God made a way for us to connect by utilizing Facetime for our sessions. God always makes a way.

Part of my inner healing included what Deirdre called vision work. My initial thoughts were, *I don't think this is going to work.* The concept just seemed so foreign to me. Even though I had some definitive doubts, I trusted her and knew she would walk me through whatever happened.

> *Walk with the wise and become wise; associate with fools and get in trouble.* (Proverbs 13:20 NLT)

Sensing my apprehension and working to put me at ease, Deirdre gently instructed me to lean back in my chair and just breathe. I had no idea what would happen. As I breathed in peace and quieted my mind, my anxiety diminished. She asked if I was ready, and I nodded.

As I focused on my healing process, I leaned back, closed my eyes, and in an instant, I was looking at the most beautiful cabin in the woods. It seemed like something out of *Lord of the Rings,* but I knew I had never laid eyes on anything like this ever before in my life. I knew it was special.

I was there but knew Deirdre was with me as well as she asked me, "Can you tell me what you see?"

So I began describing all of this to Deirdre. "I'm in front of the most beautiful cabin in the woods. Oh my gosh, there's Jesus." One minute I was hugging Jesus. The next moment, Jesus and I were outside the cabin on the right side of the house. What I saw next almost blinded me, We were standing in front of the most beautiful garden. There were flowers everywhere. The lushness of my surroundings was almost too much to take in; everything was just so big. It was the most incredible thing I had ever seen, and what I really wanted was to just stay there with Jesus and take it all in. I didn't want to leave but knew we were going to, but not yet. We were by the garden for a reason, but I had no idea what it was. The next thing I knew, He had His back to me and was on His knees. I couldn't see what He was doing at first. Then I saw. Jesus was digging with His hands. Digging into the darkest earth, it was almost black. He seemed to be trying to uncover something. It took a while before He stopped digging, and I could see He had something in His hands. But before I could see what He had, we were back in the front of the house.

I saw Jesus in front of me, walking toward someone. I couldn't make out who it was, so I decided I would get closer. I took a few steps and could see Jesus speaking to someone; again, I walked closer. Then when I could, I looked past Jesus, who again had His back to me, and saw myself looking back at Jesus. He came closer to my other me and opened His hands. What He had pulled out of the garden was there in His hands covered in that thick black dirt. I was confused and wasn't sure what was happening. Then Jesus spoke. As He spoke, he opened His hands a little wider. I could see a shape and some red color and realized that it was a heart that Jesus had unearthed. He opened His hands all the way, and as He was handing it to me, the dirt fell away, revealing a pristine perfect heart. As I took the heart in my hands, Jesus began to speak. He looked at me so lovingly and said, "Claire, I want your whole heart, and I want your heart whole." He took me in His arms as I sobbed, knowing there was still some work for me to do, but I wouldn't do it alone

> *For in time of trouble He shall hide me in His pavilion; in the secret place of His tabernacle He shall hide me; He shall set me high upon a rock.* (Psalm 27:5 NKJV)

The Heavenlies

A few weeks later, Deirdre and I connected again, and she said we were going to do some more vision work. This time, my thoughts were more positive, recalling Jesus' words to me – God was pursuing me, but He was also pursuing my healing. He understood what I had gone through and what I needed to be healed from, of that I was sure. So again, I sat, taking easy deep breaths, and then closed my eyes. This time I was with Jesus in my backyard, where I grew up.

We were outside of the family dining room, looking through a set of French doors. I started to feel anxious as the dining room wasn't a room where I ever felt safe. My chest tightened, and my breathing became more rapid, and I knew I was having a reaction due to my PTSD.

Let me give you some background. I unknowingly acquired PTSD (Post Traumatic Stress Disorder) as a child. Many people recognize the term PTSD as that which comes from a soldier being in battle, but that is not the only kind. People of all ages can acquire the disorder due to any long-lasting trauma. I had developed Complex Childhood Trauma-Induced PTSD due to abuse and neglect I experienced growing up. I needed to face this trauma to experience inner healing. And God graciously allowed Deirdre to walk through this process with me.

Our dining room table is where a lot of hurt and brokenness occurred, as my grandmother verbally brutalized me every night as I sat across from her. My brother Larry tried to sit in my seat once, so I sat in my grandfather's seat, but I was told that I wasn't worthy of sitting in my grandfather's seat, and then the reasons were listed why – not lauding my grandfather, but degrading me.

The verbal abuse started when I was around 13 years old and continually got worse until I left for college. My grandfather and grandmother had been together for 50 years when he died. My grandmother, not having a relationship with Jesus or other Christians, dropped her basket and released her grief in a manner that was destructive to all those around her. I was simply in the line of fire.

Despite the abuse and trauma, I never gave up on my grandmother or the relationship I felt we should have. When I was away at college, Mom called to tell me my grandmother had diabetes. I wasn't sure what to do, but I had enough money to send her a bouquet of daisies. Daisies were my grandmother's favorite flowers. I remember my grandfather finding daisies for her even in the dead of winter, which was no easy feat back in the day. About a week after I sent the flowers, I received a letter from her thanking me for the flowers. Included with the letter was a $20 bill for "a beer and a steak." That was her way of giving me love. This would be our correspondence while I was away at school, always ending with $20 for a beer and a steak.

God has a way of providing us with a Christian community even when that community isn't built into our home life. Looking back at the summer after junior college, I recognize that God was working in my life when He provided me with a home away from home. I spent the summer living with my godparents in Maryland and working a job teaching swimming lessons and life-guarding. I felt free and out of the craziness that I had grown up in. During this time, I also saw God's protection.

I was working at the pool and was having a great summer when my now-husband Brian (the middle son of my godparents) asked me if I had talked to my mom recently, and I hadn't. He then began to tell me about a fire that had destroyed about 50% of our home. I was devastated. It was unnerving that I had to find out about this from someone else. I called my mom, and she verified the account, saying, "Don't worry, everything is being handled." She and my grandmother were living in a hotel, waiting for a trailer to arrive that they would live in temporarily. I did go home for a weekend to see the damage, and I found out that all my belongings were destroyed by fire, smoke, or water. I was crushed, but reminded myself that they were only things, and I was thankful to God that everyone was ok, even the dog.

A few weeks later, on a day that I was off, the phone rang, and my godmother (Aunt Bobbye) answered. It was my grandmother calling to say that she felt that I should come home and take care of my family. My godmother, truly sent by God, was having none of it. I sat on the steps going down to the basement and was petrified I would be sent home. I heard the conversation getting very tense, and finally, Aunt Bobbye said, "I find it hard to believe that two grown women need a 20-year-old to drop out of college to take care of them." I could hear my grandmother yelling but couldn't understand the words. When I came up the stairs, I heard Aunt Bobbye say, "There is no way in God's green earth that I am going to send her back to babysit two adults," and then she hung up the phone.

I knew my mom would have to deal with Grandma later, so I called her at work. She was horrified about the call Grandma had made without telling her, and she agreed that my place was at school.

That was 1983; my grandmother would only live until 1985. When she died, my mother was devastated, and yes, we were all sad, but we knew it was her time. The problem was, though, that all those years of verbal abuse had damaged my self-esteem, and the lenses I now wore of how I saw myself and how I thought others looked at me had been damaged.

Trying to be good enough

Because my identity was not rooted in Christ, I wasn't rooted in anything, but I kept on trying to be good enough, which would be an exercise in futility. My redemption would only come by truly accepting Jesus as my savior, which eventually would happen, and then I could throw those old glasses away and embrace my identity as an adopted daughter of the King of the kings and Lord of lords.

Get new glasses / Spiritual glasses

> But now thus says the LORD, He who created you, O Jacob, He who formed you O Israel: Fear not, for I have redeemed you; I have called you by name, you are mine. (Isaiah 43:1 ESV)

> For we are God's masterpiece. He has created us anew in Christ Jesus, so we can do the good things he planned for us long ago. (Ephesians 2:10 NLT)

Many years later, while traveling in Europe, I was reading a book by Bobby Houston from Hillsong Church. The book, *Colour,* was a gift to all who attended the very first Colour Conference in the United States. One night while reading it, I came across a term "generational misogyny," which means the mistreatment by an older generation of women toward the younger generation of women. I stopped for a few minutes to talk to my mom about it

Cost "Aretha" Blue Miracle Movies → Cost Loved Blue Miracle

Luke Wilson → 12 mighty orphans

- we both felt the same thing. Our grandmothers had treated their daughters and granddaughters like they had no value. We vowed that night to never let the future generations be treated that way. This ugly thing had been hanging around my family for several generations, but no more. Jesus knew how that affected me.

> *Do to others as you would like them to do to you.* (Luke 6:31 NLT)

So Deirdre and I were together by Facetime, and we were sitting and breathing, and then I closed my eyes, and I looked through the French doors of my childhood dining room. I was very anxious just looking in – and now you can understand why. But then, as I sat safely in my home as an adult, remembering that room, I saw Jesus next to me – Claire, His daughter. I wasn't sure what was going to happen next, but I knew I was safe. The next thing I knew, I was sitting in my grandfather's chair at the head of the table. Grown-up-me panicked.

And then I heard Deirdre say, "Where are you?"

I answered, "I'm sitting in my grandfather's chair."

Knowing how I felt about that, she told me to take a few slow deep breaths. Then she asked me, "Claire, where is Jesus?"

"He's under the table!"

Deirdre then asked me, "What is He doing?"

I was sobbing, trying to get the words out. "He is washing my feet."

Before she could ask another question, we were no longer in the dining room.

I looked around me; everything was so bright I almost had to close my eyes. I was sitting on a very large marble throne, and Jesus was at my feet drying them off. As He did, He spoke to me, "Claire, you will always be welcome at my table, sitting right next to me," and I turned to see that He, too, was sitting on a throne, right next to me. He reached out and held my hand. "You have always been worthy, you will always be worthy, and that's what I died for." I wanted so badly to say something, but it was over. It seemed like it took a minute for all of this to happen, but in fact, it was over 15 minutes.

A few weeks later, after Deirdre and I were wrapping up our session, she said she was going to start praying, but she wanted me to close with thanks for all of the things God had revealed to me. So she prayed, and when she stopped, I began. There were many things I gave thanks for, including the fact that God had resurrected my heart out of the darkness. Like a flood, the knowledge of the two visions came together to reveal God's purpose to resurrect my heart that had been buried under so much darkness, from my childhood, up to that day. He pulled me out of the darkness into His glorious day.

> *But you are a chosen race, a royal priesthood, a holy nation, a people for God's own possession, so that you may proclaim the excellencies of Him who has called you out of darkness into His marvelous light.* (1Peter 2:9 ESV)

As a Christian, there are many things that I am thankful for. I praise God for my salvation and the fact that I have been chosen to spend eternity with Him. I thank God for His forgiveness and the second chances He has given me. And I thank Him for the abundant blessings that He showers on me and the power and wisdom with which He equips me. But one of the most important things that I thank God for is the growth process that He continually leads me through and the people He has gifted to me to gently hold my hand as I walk down that path of healing.

As we go through life, we will all be wounded and scarred. We will all have uphill battles and days that exhaust us. But as Christians, we can trust that our God is for us and He goes before us. We can trust that He will send people in our path to hold the lamp when we can't, to point us in the right direction, and to remind us that we belong to God. And there isn't anything better than that. I pray that as you walk, you will open your eyes to the community that God has gifted you with, and I pray that you will have a teachable heart and allow that community to speak life into you, by the power of Christ Himself.

> *Two are better than one, because they have a good [more satisfying] reward for their labor; For if they fall, the one will lift up his fellow. But woe to him who is alone when he falls and has not another to lift him up! Again, if two lie down together, then they have warmth; but how can one be warm alone? And though a man might prevail against him who is alone, two will withstand him. A threefold cord is not quickly broken.* (Ecclesiastes 4:9-12 NLT)

Embrace Adoration to God

by Julie T. Jenkins

Adoration. To adore. To give worship and a deep love and respect to. We are called to adore our Heavenly Father – and I submit that adoration is a reasonable response for who God is!

Perhaps you are gaining a better understanding of God's uniqueness as you read through this book. Hopefully, you are recognizing His constant love, care, and protection over the lives of each woman who has so carefully and prayerfully written her story. And it is our goal that our words are causing you to reflect on how God has worked and is working in your life. God IS everything. Let's look at some of His names that tell us so much about Him.

Jehovah Jireh. The Lord is our Provider. Think back on your life as the authors in this book have done. Where and how has God provided for you? Psalm 50:10 reminds us that God owns everything in this world, even every animal of the forest. Everything you have is a gift from God – your family, your friends, your belongings, even your wisdom and health and personality. When we meditate on just how much God has provided for us, we can't help but humbly give Him worship and thanks.

Jehovah Rapha. The Lord is our Healer. Imagine a world where healing didn't exist – where every wound and open sore remained, where we were forced to carry every emotional trauma for a lifetime. That is almost beyond our scope of understanding! We take for granted that all things are renewed in God. And we forget His power, requesting healing in the way we think best, refusing to accept that He heals perfectly, beyond what we can even imagine. When we come to Christ, giving our sinful selves to Him, our dirty rags as it were, He clothes us with His healing righteousness, and we are made perfect for eternity. When we truly absorb this, adoration for Jehovah Rapha will flow freely from every cell of our bodies.

Jehovah Raah. The Lord is our Shepherd. This name has gotten lost in time because we simply don't understand the full meaning of the word shepherd in today's culture. The shepherd stepped out of his home to enter the wilderness with his sheep, leading them to water and food, protecting them from danger, carrying them when they couldn't walk, and finding quiet pastures for them so they could rest. Does this sound familiar? Our Jesus gave up His throne in heaven to come to a dirty, sinful earth to ensure that WE were okay. And to help us find our way home. Rest your head in the deep love of our adoring Lord, and allow your love to flow back to Him.

Adonai. Our Sovereign Master. Our Lord knows all there is to know. He has control of everything ever created. And yet, this powerful Adonai, is also our...

Abba. Our Daddy. We are God's children! You are the apple of His eye! I've heard it said that if God had a wallet, your picture would be in it. If God had a refrigerator, your picture would be taped to it. He won't ever let you out of His sight, and He cares about every detail of every minute of every day of your life! And this powerful, majestic, all-knowing King of kings and Lord of lords longs for a hug from YOU. He adores YOU. As you acknowledge this, respond to Him in respect and awe.

Jehovah Tsidkenu. The Lord is Righteous. Perfect. Without fault. Do you remember the first time your mom or dad let you down? It can be devastating as a child to realize that our earthly parents are less than perfect. But God IS perfect! He will never let you down, or go back on His Word, or leave you without His wisdom and guidance. Therefore, we can rightly give Him our full worship, reverence, praise, and honor.

Adoration to God. When we ponder who God is, who He REALLY is, adoring Him is as natural as breathing! As Christians, some of what we are called to do requires stepping out, being brave and strong, and putting forth effort - but giving God His due adoration? As we grow spiritually and come to know Him better, we will realize more and more every day that to know Him is to love Him. Embrace adoration to God. He has already embraced His adoration of you!

. . . .

Wendy Arelis

lives in the beautiful city of Kelowna in British Columbia, Canada. She was married for twenty-seven years, raised two daughters, has six grandchildren and one great-grandson.

Wendy has written her memoir, *The Other Side Of Fear. My Journey Into Perfect Love* (pen name, W. Veronica Lisare), about overcoming the challenges of childhood abuse, cancer, and divorce. She was recently nominated for two Readers Magnet Festival of Storytellers Quill Awards and won The Author of the Season in the women's category.

BEING — CHOOSING — LESS THAN A PINHEAD

Wendy worked as a registered nurse in the maternity and neonatal unit for forty-two years. She also attended several ministry schools, including Youth With A Mission, A More Excellent Way, and Bethel School Of Supernatural Ministry. During her two years at Bethel, she learned an inner healing model called Sozo, which she uses to lead people into their freedom.

Wendy has been on mission trips to the West Indies, the Philippines, Israel, Mexico, and South Africa. She has served as an elder, prayer team leader, teacher, and inner healing minister in her church. Photography, traveling, and meeting new people are Wendy's passions.

PRAYER REQUESTS

1) KRISTEN - (CHERYL) Break up

2) Dierdre - A Book - struggling → (FIRE FOR CHRIST)

3) Cathy - interviews - 2 different companies — WISDOM & DISCERNMENT — CLEAR DIRECTION

4) Christy - PRAISES - FOR TIME AWAY - GRATEFUL

5) LOIS - NEUROPATHY - LEFT SIDE NOT WORKING →

6) maureen —

NO PITY PARTY

LIFE AFTER NEAR DEATH

by Wendy Arelis

Lying on my bathroom floor, desperately trying to remain conscious, I wondered if this was how my life would end. "I am only forty-five years old. Oh no! I waited too long. I should have gone for help," I thought as I chastised myself. Fear gripped me as I lay there feeling too weak to move or even call out for help. As a nurse, I instinctively knew that I needed to keep my circulating blood flowing to my brain, so I assumed the shock position with my head low and feet up on the wall. If I passed out, I could bleed to death. No one knew I had been here all night. But God! He knew. Suddenly, His firm, assuring words captured my attention. "Wendy, you have given me your life; now let me manage it!" Ah yes. That sharp reminder was necessary for me to realize that this is what my salvation was about. I needed to trust Him with my actual life! Even though I had no idea how my Lord would help me, I intentionally relaxed and surrendered my life into His hands. The familiar scripture verse drifted through my mind, ".... My grace is sufficient for you, for My strength is made perfect in weakness..." 2 Corinthians 12:9 (NKJV) And so I waited. Only a few moments passed before I heard my husband's heavy footsteps coming up the stairs. He hurriedly banged on my teenaged daughter's bedroom door, yelling, "Call 911! Get an ambulance!" Then suddenly, he was standing over me. The paramedics arrived quickly and, after taking my pulse, determined that I had lost at least half of my total blood volume.

Looking back, I realize that I took my health for granted. Working the stressful twelve-hour shifts in the nursing profession was in itself enough to be challenging. Add to that my role as a mother caring for two chronically ill daughters, serving in several ministry positions at church, and endlessly searching for marital solutions for my ailing twenty-five-year marriage. I had no idea that the annual bouts of bronchitis and pneumonia were warning signs that my immune system was weakening. Pulling up my bootstraps and powering through was what I believed was expected of me. Most of the time, I felt overwhelmed with my life. There was no room for joy or fun. As a child, I was taught that striving to achieve was our life purpose, and enjoying life was frivolous.

Fatigue plagued me, so I sought answers from a naturopath. Trusting authority figures came easily for me, and I willingly took his homeopathic solutions without question. Having had a great relationship with my medical doctor for fourteen years, I found myself perplexed and frustrated that he wouldn't refer me to see a gynecologist when I developed the unusual heavy bleeding. My people-pleasing behavior and avoiding confrontation at all costs were not, and never will be, my allies. I was shocked to hear him discount my symptoms, saying, "Oh, you women and your problems. Men have issues too!" I got the message loud and clear, "Go away and don't mention this again." And so, for nine long months, I wore a huge, bulky diaper-type pad and tried to adjust my life to the uncontrollable bleeding. Daily prayers for healing, direction, and answers were added to my already long list of requests.

But on this one critical night, the bleeding did not wane as it had before. My husband and daughter had gone to bed in their respective rooms. From ten o'clock that evening until six o'clock in the morning, I was on and off the toilet as the blood just kept pouring out. I was so very tired and only wanted to sleep. Continuing to think it would ease up soon, I thought I might try to drive myself to the hospital with a towel between my legs. The thought of asking my husband for help, disturbing his sleep, never occurred to me. Shortly before I felt faint in the wee hours of the morning, I recall having the thought, "Wow, a body can sure lose a lot of blood, and nothing bad seems to happen." Well, I was so very wrong. After arriving at the hospital, I would finally be seen by a gynecologist. There had been a series of Hepatitis B tainted blood in the recent months, so I requested not to have a transfusion if at all possible. My doctor stated that if my hemoglobin was below 60g/L, I would need to have it replaced. Praise God! My level was just that, half of the normal level. My husband left from home to go to work. I didn't see him until much later that evening when he came to pick me up. I asked him how he knew to check on me that morning, and he said that God woke him up and told him to get to me as I was in trouble! With nothing but a saline intravenous infusion, I waited alone for twelve long hours while lying on a narrow stretcher before they could do the Dilation and Curettage surgery. I don't recall being checked once while I waited in the busy hallway, but praise God, I didn't lose one more drop of blood. Upon awakening from the anesthetic, I saw two doctors' faces staring closely at me and looking perplexed. One said, "How did you not bleed out? We saw clotted blood suspended in your uterus like a big cluster of grapes."

I replied, "Do you mean how did I not bleed to death?"

They said, "Yes."

I answered, "It was God."

They answered not a word.

Thank you, Lord Jesus, for saving my life!

My surgeon called a couple of days later, saying he wanted to see my husband and me in his office. My reaction to his news telling us that I had an aggressive stage two uterine cancer wasn't alarming. My first thought was, "Finally, I know what is causing this, and it can be fixed."

I would need to have a total hysterectomy which includes removing the ovaries, fallopian tubes, and uterus. Strangely, the word "cancer" didn't make me fearful. In fact, I had an unusual joy. Was I just hoping that this crisis would be the catalyst to bring healing to our broken marriage?

Was this the "joy of the Lord" which the Bible says "is our strength"? (Nehemiah 8:10b NKJV)

My husband and I drove home in silence. He never ever spoke to me about the diagnosis. I was puzzled and didn't know how to process his silence. Was he worried? Taking my cues as to how to behave based on his reactions was how I lived my life with him. So, I just carried on, taking care of everything, as I always did. I realized that I could not lean on him at all for support. And yet, I had hope that somehow God would use this situation to heal our relationship. I would be willing to suffer anything for that.

I decided to call my regular doctor and inform him of what had happened. I hoped that my experience would encourage him to send his female patients with unusual uterine bleeding to a gynecologist. Sadly, he just responded with a legal comment, "I make no admission of wrongdoing." He must have assumed I would sue him, but no, that was not my intention. Having learned how essential it was to forgive people, I intentionally practiced it regularly when I thought of him or even saw him after returning to work.

My abdominal surgery took place two weeks after the hemorrhage. The vertical incision was extremely painful, and the recovery was slow. Already anemic, I lost more blood during the operation. It took months before my levels returned to normal. But now, I had a new problem. My body went into instant menopause due to the loss of my estrogen sources. One result was that I developed the "sweats," which went on for years. I had been told that I could possibly need radiation, and I felt disappointed when my gynecologist informed me that radiation was indeed recommended because the cancer had spread into the middle layer of the uterus. He added "It doesn't hurt, and it will be just like going to camp." Our city didn't offer the treatments, so I was required to travel to the coastal city of Vancouver, which is about a four-hour drive from where I lived. My sister and family were moving to the area where I lived, and so I wasn't looking forward to being away for the six weeks required for the radiation. Nevertheless, I assumed that God was sending me there as He wanted me to share Jesus with other cancer patients. Looking at this sacrifice as an assignment from heaven helped me to adjust to the idea. The Cancer Clinic Lodge provided me with housing and meals. Having my own car there wasn't necessary, so my husband drove me. While saying goodbye, I sensed a hint of a possible spark of love between us. However, he didn't delay his departure and seemed eager to get on the road. Even though my sister and friends tried to help in several ways, I realized that this walk with the Lord was one that only He and I could take together. A new loneliness accompanied me. My daily treatments quickly took a toll on my body, burning my intestines. After only a few days, I was unable to eat food as everything went right through me. Although I had looked forward to discovery walks and bus rides to lovely areas of this city, that became more unmanageable as I experienced the ongoing bowel bleeding and diarrhea. On the first few weekends, I took the long 5-hour ride bus home. Sadness and disappointment weighed heavily on me as my eyes searched for a joyful greeting from my husband.

Sharing a room with new women each week was challenging as I longed to find places to be alone to pray. Fibromyalgia and severe back pain, along with the interrupted sleep from the menopausal symptoms, took a toll on me. I wasn't feeling much like an ambassador for Christ. Everything in me wanted to run each time I felt forced to get up on the treatment bed to allow more radiation burning. I wasn't in the habit of asking the Lord about decisions I made. I just went along with what I was told to do and presumed it was the right decision. "Was I doing the right thing, Lord? Is this really your will?" But somehow, I thought it was too late to change my mind, so I would endure until the weeks were over. On one very difficult day, I felt like I could take no more. Since I tended to take every word I read in the Bible literally, I thought of King Hezekiah and how he asked God to grant him fifteen more years to live. (2 Kings 20: 1-5) Believing that if God was going to use this cancer to turn my marriage around, I wanted to be here to experience it. So, I prayed and asked God to grant me the same number of years. Thankfully, God didn't answer that prayer exactly as that would have only brought me to age sixty. Presently, I am enjoying twenty-six years cancer-free! Praise you, Lord! He has numbered my days here on earth.

My sister and her husband hosted my husband each evening, serving him a lovely gourmet meal. I could hear the laughter in the background as I spoke on the phone with her. Although I was very grateful for their gift of hospitality, I wondered if my husband missed me or was even concerned. I rarely heard him laugh in our home. Back pain plagued him. Some nights he would venture down to the basement guest room to sleep in a bed that he found more comfortable. With my shiftwork and unusual sleep schedules, living in separate rooms had become our normal for the past ten years. We were drifting further apart and rarely even ate a meal together. On many mornings, he would get up and go out somewhere without saying a word. My heart yearned for companionship, but whenever I brought it up, he got angry and stormed out of the room. Silence and avoiding conflict seemed to be the foundation of our relationship.

Finally, my graduation day arrived. After one more internal radiation treatment, I was done. Hallelujah! My husband surprised me by sending me a dozen red roses. Hope arose in me again.

Traveling home by air was a welcomed relief, although managing all of my accumulated belongings was challenging. I prayed that my bowels would behave as I waited in the lineups.

After I arrived home, visiting my sister and family several times a week was such a welcomed blessing. I enjoyed her lovingly prepared meals as well as our heart-to-heart talks. My gynecologist set up regular check-ups with him for five years. He told me that this cancer was fed by estrogen, so I wasn't eligible for hormone replacement therapy. Searching for natural alternatives to treat my menopausal symptoms became a seemingly endless and expensive venture. One day I decided to look at the ingredients of the homeopathic solution I had been taking for many months. I was horrified to see that it contained estrogen! "Oh Lord, could this have caused the cells in my uterus to multiply at such a rapid rate?" Of course, the naturopath denied it when I asked him, but I am convinced it contributed to this cancer. I berated myself for being so gullible and not seeking the Lord before taking treatments. Hearing His voice did not come easily for me. Frustration and unbelief tormented me when I sought Him for answers to my questions. The silence was a sign of rejection I knew only too well. I didn't like feeling like a failure. It reminded me of when I was a student at school. "Everyone else understands the math except you," the enemy taunted. I believed the lie that I was stupid and not capable of learning. "What was I doing wrong? Why can't I hear You? Are You angry with me and ignoring me, God?" I thought. Years later, I would understand that as I pursue an intimate relationship with Him, He has various ways of communicating with me. My faith to hear continues to grow.

As I had done many times before, I intentionally forgave the naturopath whenever I felt anger towards him. As well, I needed to have grace for myself for making this careless mistake. Learning the hard way seemed necessary for me to grow. I didn't really think about how the enemy wants to "steal, kill and destroy." (John 10:10a NKJV)

After several months passed, the hospital began to inquire when I would be returning to work. The thought of going back to shiftwork was frightening as I believed that the stress of those twelve-hour shifts contributed to this sickness. The doctors caring for me had not advised me when I should return. I reluctantly agreed to a program of gradually returning to work six months after the hemorrhage. My co-workers greeted me warmly and were very supportive. I was unprepared for the emotional breakdown that I would have only two hours into my shift. What was happening to me? I wasn't naturally a weeping woman, but here I found myself unable to hold back the unexplainable tears. My supervisor quickly sent me home with the admonition to "come back when you are ready to work."

Another harsh reaction greeted me from my husband as I entered our home. I was shocked and unprepared for his angry outburst when I desperately needed comfort and understanding. Why is he so angry? "Dear Lord, what is happening to me?" I cried. I have always been able to manage my emotions. My new family doctor offered no solutions. He suggested I apply for a psychiatric disability, which made me feel like he didn't understand at all what I was going through. Thankfully, the Holy Spirit led me to another doctor who was a knowledgeable, compassionate believer in Christ. He kindly asked me why I was trying to go back to work so soon. Apparently, patients like me should be off work for two years. Thank you, Lord, for your abundant grace. It was a relief to know that my body simply needed more time to balance out my hormones.

Gradually, over the years, my body has indeed become accustomed to not having estrogen. Healing for my intestines has been a longer, slower process, and I continue to contend for their complete restoration. Sadly, my marriage ended two years after the cancer diagnosis. The most devastating moment of my life was when I discovered my husband's adultery. My value seemed to shatter into a million pieces. I was grieved to the very depths of my soul. But

God held me. He carried and provided all that I needed through the months to come. He is faithful.

I have now lived a single life for the past twenty-four years, which would not have been my first choice, but they have been rich years of discovery, growing in faith, overcoming fears, and pursuing God's purpose for my life. Untethered, I am free to live as a favoured daughter of the King of kings. I can honestly say that these last years have been the most rewarding ones of my whole life. I am thankful to God for giving me more time here on earth to serve Him and share my story.

Be encouraged, dear reader; God is for us and will take what the enemy intended for evil and turn it for good. It is in the raging storms of our life that our faith is really tested. During those times, He shows Himself faithful as long as we trust Him. When fear grips you, declare out loud, "Jesus I trust you! Have mercy on me!" Lamentations 3:22-23(NKJV) says "Through the Lord's mercies we are not consumed, because His compassions fail not. They are new every morning; great is your faithfulness." Praying scriptures such as Psalm 46:1 (TPT) builds our faith and draws us close to Him. "God, you're such a safe and powerful place to find refuge! You're a proven help in time of trouble-more than enough and always available whenever I need you." Give Him your whole life. He can be trusted with it.

Embrace Leadership

by Julie T. Jenkins

We are all called to leadership - you may lead a Fortune 500 company, your family, or you most likely lead somewhere in the middle. The fact is that we each have many different leadership roles and experiences throughout our lifetime.

The Bible teaches that leadership is a necessity. Proverbs 11:14 (NLT) states, "Without wise leadership, a nation falls." We can swap out the word nation with business, community, ministry, or even family. As Christians, God assures us that He will equip and empower us to lead where He calls us, but we still have an obligation to continually learn and grow so that we can be effective in our role as a leader.

Two necessary elements of good leadership are having a servant's heart and listening well.

First and foremost, a good leader will serve others. Jesus taught and modeled this, even washing the feet of His disciples in humble service. (John 13) In Galatians 5:13, Paul teaches, "You have been called to live in freedom...use your freedom to serve one another in love." (NLT) Being a servant-leader means having the willingness to put the interest of others before our own, thinking of others before we think of ourselves, and, while graciously depending on the help of others, never considering ourselves "above" others or refusing to do work that may seem "beneath" us.

It is a normal human flaw to want to be greater than others, but that is a tendency we must guard against. When the disciples got into a discussion about which one of them would be greater, Jesus taught them, "Whoever wants to be first must take last place and be the servant of everyone else." (Mark 9:35 NLT)

Second, a good leader must listen well. In Matthew 15:13, after Jesus shared a parable, Peter asked Jesus to explain the meaning. Jesus listened and responded. A good leader will listen to those he or she leads, building an environment where each individual is appreciated as the leader learns from different perspectives. If God put you in a leadership position for a purpose, you can bet that He also put those serving under you in position for a purpose. And part of their responsibility is to share from their vantage point while the effective leader listens. When we don't listen to others, we devalue them and turn away a gift of knowledge supplied by God.

Beyond listening well to others, we must also listen well to the One who knows all things and is willing to give us His wisdom. As a leader, God expects you to turn to Him in every decision to help you lead the people He loves so dearly! Psalm 37:5 teaches, "Commit everything you do to the Lord. Trust him, and he will help you." (NLT)

Jesus Christ was the best leader who ever walked the face of the earth – we would do well to follow His example and have His attitude! So as you lead, make it your priority to be a servant and listen well!

. . . .

Afterword

There was nothing easy about the Israelites journey to the Promised Land. But God provided.

On their obedient trek to birthing the Christian church, the disciples persevered through joys and trials. And God gave them the strength.

And despite not knowing where God was taking him, Abraham became the father of many nations by the power and plan of God.

As we read the Bible, it is often the stories that speak to us, reminding us that if God did it for someone else, He can do it for us, too. And the stories that we've shared with you in this book have been written for the same reason – to give God the glory and to give you hope as you embrace your journey to spiritual growth. So, as you close this book, I want to encourage you to persevere on the path God has you. But don't just persevere. Walk the path expectantly, seeking God's glory! He has a plan that is better than you can ask or imagine, and He is just waiting for you to take hold of it! As you do, don't forget to write it all down. You don't want to ever forget, and one day, if you let Him, God will use your testimony to inspire someone else to walk, run, or even soar!

Have you never heard?
Have you never understood?
The Lord is the everlasting God,
the Creator of all the earth.
He never grows weak or weary.
No one can measure the depths of his understanding.
He gives power to the weak
and strength to the powerless.
Even youths will become weak and tired,
and young men will fall in exhaustion.

But those who trust in the Lord will find new strength.
They will soar high on wings like eagles.
They will run and not grow weary.
They will walk and not faint.
(Isaiah 40:28-31 NLT)

Prayer Requests

8/10/00

1. Cheryl —
   — Daughter's Boyfriend Broke up w/ her —
   She's a mess, Pastor Craig → Kristen pray for her.
   Cheryl — pray for her → Available

2. Christy →
   PRAISE → visit son girlfriend →
   Christy gone (Saturday) → Not

3. Maureen — Health —
   Surg. To pray to mention
   Available

4. LOIS → Health.

5. Lauren — Daughter → job perfection →
   ← → Perfect plan

7/8/22

→ LOIS - SWITCH → SABRINA
  TIRED → HOURS - HONORS
  → NURSING SCHOOL
  → KROUSE → LOCATION
→ WILLING-cough → COURT
  RESOLUTION / move FOWARD
  PAIN mgmt   PLAN.

Deirdre - GODLY WISDOM
KEIRA - soften her heart.

Cheryl -
Sleeping Better/
MASK.
Katelyn - job - interview
  Jordan Donuts -
Brewing - Daughter / Kristin

Cathy - PRAISE Set a boundary
Tommy Howe - Found Safely
GoDly WISDOM -
Ex wants To get back together

✓ Christy ✓ 2/1/22

✓ Lois ✓

✓ Lauren ✓

✓ Deidre

✓ Cheryl

✓ Cathey Johnson ? (Chicago) (Bucay - Dave) (28 years → "River Bridge")
→ Tony Howe

✓ Carlene Foley

• Lauren — NC/ Details
- Lois - Sabrina - Pray → condition/Heart
- Christy - Continued prayers for Direction/wisdom
- Dierdre - Friends
  Tom/Dad
  mom
  → COVID
  Kiera - Heart surgery for Lord!
  Test for work/
  Bible Study - Prayer

— Cheryl - Sleep / New job 8pm-9am
  (Pray for sleep)

— Cathy - Praises being lead to this Group

Made in the USA
Columbia, SC
03 December 2021

→ Karen Brown
→ Hardgar

50083263R00157